God's Imagination

The Loving Light Books Series

Book 1: God Spoke through Me to Tell You to Speak to Him
Book 2 & 3: No One Will Listen to God & You are God
Book 4: The Sun and Beyond
Book 5: The Neverending Love of God
Book 6: The Survival of Love
Book 7: We All Go Together
Book 8: God's Imagination
Book 9: Forever God
Book 10: See the Light
Book 11: Your Life as God
Book 12: God Lives
Book 13: The Realization of Creation
Book 14: Illumination
Book 15: I Touched God
Book 16: I and God are One
Book 17: We All Walk Together
Book 18: Love Conquers All
Book 19: Come to the Light of Love
Book 20: The Grace is Ours

Also by Liane Rich

The Book of Love
For the Love of God: An Introduction to God
For the Love of Money: Creating Your Personal Reality
Your Individual Divinity: Existing in Parallel Realities
For the Love of Life on Earth
Your Return to the Light of Love: a guidebook to spiritual awakening

Loving Light

Book 8

God's Imagination

Liane Rich

The information contained in this book is not intended as a substitute for professional medical advice. Neither the publisher nor the author is engaged in rendering professional advice to the reader. The remedies and suggestions in this book should not be taken, or construed, as standard medical diagnosis, prescription or treatment. For any medical issue or illness consult a qualified physician.

Loving Light Books

ISBN 13: 978-1-878480-08-8
ISBN 10: 1-878480-08-1

Loving Light Books:
www.lovinglightbooks.com

Also Available at:
Amazon: www.amazon.com
Barnes & Noble: www.barnesandnoble.com

for C.J.

The information in this series is not necessarily meant to be taken literally. It is meant to *shift* your consciousness....

Foreword

Anyone immersed in the vast body of new metaphysical knowledge is aware of the virtual symphony of voices from channeled sources throughout the world – inspirational voices that may be artistic, poetic, philosophical, religious, or scientific. And now, out of these myriad New Age voices, comes a series of books by God, channeled through Liane, revealing the frank truth in all its glory and wonder, telling us how to cleanse our bodies, gain access to our subconscious minds, clear our other selves and march back to who we are – God.

In God's books you will be introduced to a loving, powerful, gripping, exciting, and often humorous voice that reaches out and speaks ever so personally to the individual reader. As the reader's interest deepens, invariably an intimate relationship to this voice develops. It is a relationship that lasts forever, and I am quite certain I do mean forever.

Here is an accelerated program, a no-holds-barred course, where God guides us and loves us, and as needs be recommends books to us and even a movie or musical piece along the way. He (She) enters our lives and sees through our eyes, seeming to enjoy the ride as He guides us back to US, back to ALL. Here is a voice that is playful and informative, that is humorous and serious, that is gentle and powerfully divine. It is a voice that knows no barriers or restrictions, a straightforward and honest voice that caresses us when we need the warmth and pushes us when we are immobilized.

In today's New Age literature there is an avalanche of information from magnificent beings of light, information that possesses us and compels us to look at our fears and express our love. In this series of books by God, you will find truly powerful methods for making this transition from toxicity to purity, from density to light, from fear to love, and from the delusion of death to the awakening to full life. You will experience in these books the love and the power of God for it is your love to express and your power to behold. Rarely will you see more lucid steps for transformation. Read these beautiful words and rejoice in our period of awakening, our return to Home.

John Farrell, PhD., LCSW. – Psychologist, Clinical Social Worker, Senior Clinician Psychiatric Emergency Services, U.C. Davis Medical Center, Sacramento. John is also a retired Professor – California State University, Sacramento, in Health Sciences and Psychology.

God’s Imagination

Introduction

So far it is not so difficult to see how you have gotten a little off track. You began to believe that you were separate from God and now you can't seem to believe that *you* have any role in God's creation. How could this have occurred? How can it be that you who *are* God have completely begun to *resist* the notion that you did this to you? You blame God for pestilence and plague and death and even shout "hallelujah" when you win something big. You thank God for your good and blame God for your bad.

Most of you do not want to begin to "accept" that this God that you blame for pestilence and disease and even "floods" is actually *you.* You did this *all* to your own selves. You took over creation and made it what it is. You are God and you have created so much and traveled so far that you cannot remember how or even "why" you began all this.

This book will give you some clues as to why and I may even tell you a few new things about your past that you have forgotten. Mostly I wish to begin by welcoming you back to my school of learning – God's school. You are permitted to learn and to grow and to do whatever is necessary for you to achieve the wisdom that is your own identity. So far we have learned a great deal and I'm certain that we have all gained insight and clarity as well as some vast confused feelings about our existence on this particular plane.

Most of you are ready for healing and often this healing does not feel so good. You are being stretched and pulled and pushed-at to move and grow and change. I know this feels uncomfortable and even painful at times, but this growth is actually good. It *is* God recognizing God, God seeing his own identity, and God *allowing* himself to be born.

No one is available to God without consent. You scream and holler to be forgiven so you won't be punished for your sins. Now I come along on my white steed to say "there are no sins" and you freak out. "How can we control our universe without rules and regulations?" you shout! "How can we enforce our rules without punishment for breaking these rules?" And "who is going to save us from ourselves, because we all know how base and bad and violent we really are?" *Judgment is not how you will see heaven!* Judgment stops and even backs up the flow of life.

My concern at this time is for your safety. You have taken "on" too much energy and now I must ignite you enough to reverse spin, so that I may begin to enter you as well as enter myself. God is reconnecting with God. He is bringing you back into position so that he may enter you and become you. You are to stay put and allow all to occur. By stay put I do not mean stay in one place. I do mean stay "level." There is a "level" of vibration which is going out at this time and in order for us to be equal to one another it is best to take part in all that feels good and not get involved if it does not feel good.

So far you are very well aware of the fact that something must be occurring for all this excitement to be affecting earth. We have eruptions and shakes and quakes and fires and wind and flood. It is good! It is *life* clearing her throat in order to express in a better way. No one will leave earth without prior *acknowledgment* on their part. It's good to go, it's good to stay. Nothing is horrible, nothing is bad and nothing is wrong. Accept it and it becomes (simply what) *"is."*

*Now and then you begin to wonder at who you are and what you are really here for. Most of you believe that you simply live and play and work and grow and die. That's not why you came. You came to hide and you came to change. Most of you are on your second, third or fourth trip by now. Few of you have traveled through this entire dimension more than a dozen life times.

I know this seems unbelievable. After all, you have "seen" your past lives and you have *experienced* memory from them. You are not the sum total of your past lives. You may be hypnotized and see many past lives, because you are *all one.* Not one of you is separate from the whole. So, when you experience a *focus* on a certain life, this focus is just your (one) perception. The other you's are also *focused* on certain lives and even certain events. Most of what you see is not what occurred, but what you perceived to be correct.

So, how do we connect to our other selves and other Gods? We begin to look at *all* and to allow everything in you to be just as it is. Right now is a very crucial time for you in this dream that you call reality. Why do I feed you information while you sleep? It is to wake you gently so you do not go berserk when the lights go on. You are so accustomed to your dark room that should I walk in and turn on a bright light, you would have a very grouchy attitude and a very bad time of it. So, I am entering your dark room quietly and whispering in your ear slowly and softly.

You are not who and what you dream. You are not a focal point of creation… you *are* the light that creates. So, for now I will tell you gently that you do not have past, you do not have present, and you do not have future. What you do have is *you*. Nothing, absolutely nothing else is here. You are not the sum total of this life or any other life. *It is the illusion!* You walked onto the set of your own dream and cannot get out of this dream.

So, from this standpoint or focal point, I want you to *perceive* how nothing that you do, act out or say, is or could be in anyway harmful – not to you, not to anyone else. Without rules you will not fall apart. Without regulations you will not end and without God you do not end. How can you believe that you could be less than "God on high" when you are actually that very same God? You pray and pray for salvation and salvation is what you already have. You are not this pretender who *walks* in your dream. You *are* the dreamer, and all that you can dream now belongs to you. Hence, we have our onion to peel. Layers upon layers of God's imagination at work. None of it is real; none of it means anything of any importance.

I know that this is a very painful pill to swallow. God teaches you to be good and love one another and then he turns around and says, "None of this was of any significance." *I do not judge you and I never will.* You may hate me or love me. You may hate man or love man... it does not matter. The reason that it does not matter is that it is not real. None of it exists, so why bother. The only reason I intervene at this time is to assist you, because this nightmare of a dream is creating so much pain that you are screaming out in your sleep. God is outside of you holding you and whispering, "it's okay, you won't die" or, "it's okay, there are no bad guys" or, "it's okay, you cannot get hurt it's only a bad dream."

Do not *judge* this information as bad or wrong. I know you have many who have written on the subject of hatred and love and even reincarnation. So what! None of it "is," but all of it exists on some level of creation. It is simply nothing to get excited or judgmental about. This is one of our biggest problems on planet earth – how to get you to stop judging or going into denial on everything. Absolutely everything exists somewhere (even if it's just in *your* dream).

No one is absent from this dream because it is part of the creation story. No one creates without another, in some way, being involved. So far you have not come very far in your evolution towards your goal and so you have not much capacity for understanding what you cannot see or prove. Later on you will develop your psychic and clairvoyant abilities to the extent that you will see more readily. In some cases you will simply know or understand more readily. God's dream is not a bad dream, it is just that you got too caught up in it and began to believe *in* it.

So, now I must explain why all the emphasis in earlier books regarding clearing past lives and cleansing your bodies. If this does not matter then why bother? It is to assist you in this waking process. *You are each the exact same being.* You wrote a rule so it becomes your all-one-of-you rule. Now I must teach you that this rule is unnecessary because you only wrote it for one. No one else is here. It is like having a rule and enforcing it on each individual body part. You make your toes obey this rule and you make your fingers obey, and you push at any body part that won't obey. So now we have your fingers working on learning to walk with your feet and your toes learning to work with your hands. Your feet have toes for a purpose and *instinctively* they know how to work. Your fingers work on their own just fine.

Leave all your body parts alone to do what they were created for. No rules are ever necessary. Every part of the body is so oppressed and upset because they were created to function in a certain manner and now all of their creative, instinctual behavior has been stifled and shut-up. No one is allowed to *be*. They are *told* by another how to be and how to act and even how to obey. Most of you have shut-up your natural guidance and instinctual drive altogether. It is too confusing to *know* that you were meant to be someone, but have been pushed to be what the rules tell you to be.

So once again, what difference does it make and why does it matter? It doesn't matter. It will only help to wake you up and sooner or later you will each open your eyes and *see.* No one is here to hurt you and no one is here to punish you. You are the only one here and even you are not really here. You are simply me and I want you to wake up and remember who and what you are.

So far I have talked a great deal about separation, and of course, the light and the dark. Dark is not bad it's just not where you want to be when you have so much to do. You like being light and you like being dark. To sleep is good fun and most of you are over your fear of the "wookies" who come into your rooms at night. You are no longer a frightened child. You are ready to know that you are alone and it's okay to not be part of that huge family you thought you were part of. Your fingers and toes do make good friends, but it's okay now to know that they are just you and you really don't need to separate yourself just to have a playmate. It's okay to be *one.* It's okay to laugh and sing and dance, and it's okay to be alone when you laugh and sing and dance. Sensory stimulation is just that – stimulation. You have been here sleeping now for a very long time and I will still be waiting when you wake up because I am you.

So far it has not been good to be God. A great deal

of pain seems to be involved in your belief system. Most often you do not like to change how you view all that exists. Most of you are so busy being right that you have no room for wrong. God is all. God is right and God is wrong. Without one there could not be the opposite or other side. No part of creation is outside of God. So; in this situation regarding right and wrong, one must wonder what the difference is and why all the concern over being one or the other.

God is right. Good is right. Babies are right. Animals are right and people are wrong. This pretty much sums it up. Babies always come first because you say so and of course animals run a close second. So why do people, grown adults, have no say over their own destiny? Why do adults make animals and babies so much more "valuable" than themselves?

Most of you have this distorted belief that animals have some special "need" for protection, when in actuality they do quite fine without you. They do not require you to protect them and to save them. Now; I realize that man kills, but you must realize that animals also kill. There is a chain or balance to creation. When killing occurs in one area of creation, life is populated in another. When you begin to interfere in this natural flow you are taking the responsibility of life for the animal you protect. You are creating a void in the natural flow of creation and allowing only what *you* believe is important, to be saved. Leave these decisions to God. God is in charge of creation and I do not care to see you fighting over what animal is important and must be spared. Most animal rights activists are simply protecting themselves by protecting frightened or trapped animals.

The law of the jungle or the laws of nature have always included death and destruction. This is not wrong! It is not bad. It simply is. Stop trying to take on the world and allow everything to balance on its own. I do not wish to go into the details of how you change what was not meant to be changed by interfering in these areas. So far you have put a great deal of time and judgment into how animals are treated or mistreated. I wish to stop all judgment and get you to change how you "see" everything! Everything is actually from the light, but you are so intent on seeing bad, or judging everything as wrong, that you are creating far greater consequences for yourselves.

You do not need to get so involved. I am trying to wake you up and get you out of this dream, and all you want to do is get more involved by creating more dense energy to surround you. When you can slowly wake and come out of this state of unconsciousness you will have "risen." To rise is divine. Simply rise above it all. You have no problem watching two bugs fight it out over a piece of grain so why watch "larger" forms and freak out to stop them. Leave and let every thing alone to do what must be done. They each know how to survive if that is their natural course. No one is punished by dying. Death is simply a doorway back to God. How can a doorway home be anything so awful as you make it out to be?

So far there are too many judges and not enough

who wish to simply witness. Everyone wants to call the shots and control what goes on. No one seems to know how to simply *be* and allow all else to simply be. You are so stimulated by your anger that you use your anger to motivate you to action. Stop for a moment and discern between right and wrong. Does it matter if something is right or wrong? No... it does not. It simply *is,* in God's eyes. Leave my creation alone so that you may come out of it and return to my waiting arms. The more *involved* you become in any part of this action oriented dream, the longer it will take to wake you up. Leave it alone. Leave everything alone. Nothing is good. Nothing is bad. Nothing is right. Nothing is wrong.

This does tend to take a little getting used to on your part, but I assure you that you will rise higher and faster without carrying this dream with you. So come with me now... wake up! Give up your dream and join God outside this dream and I shall show you the true reality that is waiting for you. Don't get deeper involved in this dream. It does not really exist and you are putting all your energy into it. Take your energy back. Take your power back. Pull up stakes and leave. Leave the dream and come back to God. Meet your true self. Do not fight to hold on to any part of this dream. As long as you are playing in it you *are* in it.

*N*ow then; I wish to acknowledge the fact that no one is any better than anyone else. No one and nothing on the creation scale has any rights over or privileges over another. We are all equal in God's eyes. Bug is equal to man. Insect is equal to baby and birth is equal to death. No privileges! None. Man created these lies about how creation began and man continues to lie to himself and force this truth on others.

There is no pecking order in God's creation. You are so stuck in this dream that you have literally "fallen" into it. Thus we have a rumor of a "fallen" state of grace. So far you are not who you believe yourself to be and you are not living in a real world. You are God not man. You are dreaming not living. You are so far from truth that you now fight over the truth, but what you actually fight over is control of this dream. God's imagination is out of control and spinning and spinning. Now I wish to stop the spin and arise to begin again. God does not kill. God does not punish. God simply stops this dream from time to time. He is not an ogre.

God is love and God does not wish to continue without you. You are invited to take on the light of truth. Stop dreaming that you have any separation of status. Stop behaving as though some are totally innocent and others not. Stop protecting your right to be. You are so afraid of not "getting" your share or having your right piece of this dream that you constantly fight to "keep" you safe in your position. I do not want you safe. I need you flexible and willing to let go of your hold on your rights. The more you hold on to, the deeper into this dream you spiral. Let go of all that is and allow all that is not yet allowed in to come in. It is simply the truth arriving. Are you so afraid of truth that you must kill or persecute those who speak it?

There is a very fine line between imagination and life. Life imitates imagination and imagination imitates life. No one is here to be frozen here on earth. No one is meant to stay. This is a ride on a machine that takes you up-up-up and down-and-around. You are not meant to be stuck on this ride. You are not meant to not get off the ride. It is a game. Stop being so caught up in a game. Stop fear and judgment. Fear and judgment take you deeper into this game. Stop seeing everyone as a control device. You want to change and wake up, so you control others to stop them from hurting you, when in actuality they have not the ability to hurt you.

Come out of your television set. You have gone berserk and jumped inside to play out the movie you once sat and watched. Come out of it! Wake up. Listen to me. You are not who you think you are. You are meant to flow, not stop and fight for your rights. Continue to fight to keep what is yours and you will be allowed to keep it. You will be allowed to stay *in* the dream. But; if you choose to wake up you will move on to the light. You will rise up out of this entire situation. It only takes "belief." One little thought can begin to change this dream and allow you to come out of it. It is not truth. Nothing that you see or experience here is real.

So; why all the hoopla about getting out of the dream? It is to show you who you are. You are like this giant sleeping beast who is beginning to claw at his own body as he sleeps. Someone must wake this sleeping beast. He is not having fun on the ride he chose, so now it's time to get him off the ride. It's really that simple. No one enjoys this game anymore and all the players are fighting over the rules and regulations of a game for sleepers. Wake up and stay calm. Peace is willing to come, but it, as all energy, needs an opening. You must begin to open to all. Absolutely everything must be allowed in. It is not possible to stop this illusion without telling you what it is, because you are so caught up in it that you want to keep it. Give it away to God. Turn everything back to God. Give your power to awaken to God. Allow God to know that you know he is you. Allow God to enter the dream long enough to expose it for what it is.

So far it is not possible to show you just how far you have yet to go to return home. This journey you undertook is quite an accomplishment and yet it is nothing. You went into the unknown and became so much a part of it that now you want to return to the known, but don't know or remember how. You are so accustomed to not seeing that you now guard your blindness with guns and knives and picket signs and protest signs and contracts and any other weapon you can imagine. You are so afraid of not getting or not having that you must always "fight" for more. Did you ever stop to think what might become of you if you stayed with less instead of fighting for more?

Less is not bad. I am trying to show you a way out, and it is okay to not have. It is okay to not set goals. It is okay to not have so much as others, and most importantly it is okay to let go and "enjoy" not having. It is not wrong to have, but it is okay to not have. Most of you are so afraid of letting go of your stuff that your stuff actually weighs you down. You think of moving but you have too much stuff to move. You think of travel but who will mind the store and protect your stuff.

So far the villain is not stuff. The villain seems to be money. How can you possibly live without money in the bank, and business to make more money? This *need* on earth for money is all blown out of proportion, to the extent that those who live have money and those who lose their money eventually die in the gutter. This is not an exactitude, of course, but you get the idea. To have money is to have life and health. To not have money is to have death and disease.

Now; most of you are very, very afraid of losing your money. It is your security. I want to bring you back to a state of mind that depends on God not on money, and on love not on protection from loss. This is a very big job since you are so *convinced* that money exists and that you exist.

So far it has been most difficult to channel this information, for even my pen believes she *needs* money to survive. The truth is "the money will always come from somewhere." It is part of creation and it flows until it is blocked or no longer needed. I must get you to stop putting so much fear behind having it or not having it. It is just paper and coin. It is the base of your economy as God is the base of your spirituality. It is not necessary outside this dream, and once you wake up a little you will see how it is no more powerful than you make it.

Most of you are so afraid of not having money that you hide it and horde it. I am asking you to take some of it and spend it or give it away. See how it feels to have a little less. See how it returns to you in some other energy form. Creation is set up to flow. Where there is an opening there is a space for something, or someone to arrive. Give up to get. Stop holding on to money for dear life. Allow money to be just another thing like a dish or towel. It is not so important and it is not your savior. You are so confused that you believe your savior to be green. He is not. He is standing here telling you that God will save you from this state of affairs. No, God does not buy you much, but God does love all. Love can out-power money once you bring your power back out of money and put it back in God.

God does not wish to upset his children by taking away their security blanket so he is asking you to start giving it up a little here, a little there. If I took it from you,

you would only suffer the pain and confusion and blame me. I have done this before and it did not work. So this time I will allow you to give up freely when you feel grown up enough to do so. God does not wish to punish or hurt you, he only wants you to wake up to the fact that you are simply God, not human. You are God. This is not your true reality and it's time you gave it up. Stop being so afraid to live.

It is okay to not be what is *considered* successful in your world. Do you really think it is important to God that you succeed in making more money? Think about it. You base your beliefs on money and you scare those who do not have it by teaching that they are less. So now we have schools full of children being taught how to make more money, when in actuality they are never meant to. They are meant to be love and light and peace and joy.

Now it is time to describe your view on children. You believe you are nothing without the children. You are not nothing without your children. The world does not evolve around a child as you believe.

You began to procreate in order to "stay" in this dimension. An heir became a very important asset; someone to inherit the throne. Someone to pass the "holdings" on to, or better put, someone to leave your stuff to. A small version of you who could continue to rule and take care that the family didn't die out. Pass on the family name and all that. You did not wish to leave this dream world without leaving something or someone behind to show that you had been here.

Now it has gotten so blown out of proportion that you now convince others that life is not worth living if you do not procreate. To have a child is no more a blessed event than to have sex. It is just a bodily function that you have created and developed for this purpose. You are not wrong to create a child and you are not wrong to not create a child. It is simply a way for a new spirit to enter form. It makes no difference what so ever if you do or if you don't.

Most of you no longer realize what you are doing. You continue to procreate out of habit. It brings you peace of mind, or draws your loved one closer to you. The biggest problem with this theory is that it is incorrect. Owning a child is responsibility of another. It takes time and money. Money must then be worked for and goals set and achieved. With all this going on it is usually necessary for mom to now work also. Now I have a couple who are so "stuck" in matter by their choice to procreate that I will not receive their attention for several years. You are too busy making babies and raising babies and protecting unborn babies to give God much thought. Oh yes, you get all excited about the miracle of birth and scream hallelujah, but I want you to know or realize what this part of creation is all about. You believe in death so you decided to leave part of you behind in name only. This part that is left behind to rule or reign over your belongings is simply a fragment of your own consciousness.

Now; if you contain a great deal of physical pain, or emotional pain, or mental pain it is most likely projected onto your fragmented self. Your fragment then grows up to face you and begins to dysfunction, as he or she carries your original pain, or belief in pain. When your child reaches a certain age, and if the pain that you carry is great, your child will carry your burden of pain and be dysfunctional in some manner. Do not blame the children for rebelling. They are in pain and it was handed down to them by you. Your pain was fragmented and now exists in your fragmented self.

Now; just because you have conditioned yourself to handle pain in a certain manner does not mean that the fragment you created will handle, or "express" his or her pain in the same way. He or she is not you. He or she is *part* of you. He may begin to explode with rage, while you are the type who withdraws and comforts yourself when your pain is too great. Each individual cell within God's body is created to release and reform. If you are lucky your child, or fragment, will develop the craft or art of reforming, or using pain to heal and not destroy.

So far pain is so out of control that you *use* it to control one another. If you cause enough pain someone will listen or pay attention. If you hurt someone badly enough they will not bother you or harm you. You even hurt your mate in order to control him or her. You punish them for misbehaving by doing something that you know bothers them. This of course is self-inflicted pain, as we all know that no one can really hurt us.

So; now we have you procreating and passing your pain down through generation after generation, and now today kids are killing kids and killing parents and killing teachers and guess where it all started? At home with you. You are not functioning from a love base. *You* are the children, not some baby you create to make you feel better. Inside of you is a child; gentle, loveable and very, very hurt. Do not create more pain by fragmenting yours. Let all pain begin to heal. Allow you to heal before you take on more responsibility.

Some of you are so addicted that you shop to feel good about who you are. Some create great success to feel good about who you are. Some (most) dull their senses with stimulants or alcohol to feel good about who they are, and others have more children just to feel good about who they are. Creating life is very heady stuff. It is of the ego, and the ego enjoys the thrill of power that accompanies reproducing life. It feels good I know, but you are actually spreading you and all that you contain into them and they will pass it on.

Now it is time to begin to show you how you really came to earth and who and what you really are. You are not who you believe. You are not human. You were meant to be kings who ruled over matter and what is now occurring is quite the opposite. You are sheep being led around by the nose. You no longer use your will power to create from natural instinct.

You are in such a state of change that it is most difficult to reach you. You believe in love yet you do not know what it is. You believe that love is something that only happens in families or between mates. This is not correct. Love goes out to you from God. You then share love with all creation. Love does not begin with you and reach out to only those whom you believe deserve it.

Most of you are so confused that you believe selectiveness to be love. You select one partner and put your trust and faith in him or her and expect them to be loyal to you, and not share any of the same experiences with any stranger that they share with you. This is not love. This is privacy. It is not loyalty, it is ownership. To own a husband or a wife is not the same as love. Ownership and playing by the rules to keep your mate happy is compromise, not love.

So; what is love and how did it get so confused with need and want and desire? Love is white light energy that allows you to accept everything. When you get to the level of ascension where you can accept all by allowing it to simply be, then you will know love. Love does not feel like judgment. Judgment says, "You must only sleep with me or you are not meant to be loved by me." Love says, "I will love you unconditionally and only in this moment." You began to hold on to love so tightly that you now suffocate it by your rules. Think very carefully. Does it take only two people to transfer love just to each other, or does it require each cell loving all other cells? And how do you love and who knows they are in love and not simply hooked on someone, or in great need of a protector, or simply in a state of loneliness?

Stop judging one another for choices of separation and divorce. Two people were never meant to be locked in by rules and regulations and fear. You are simply angels flowing in spirit, not prisoners of a contract. Allow nature to flow by allowing all to simply be. It is not such a bad thing as you believe. You become moralistic and judgmental where issues of sex and mating are concerned, as you are afraid. Fear of loss. Fear of losing your own mate. I have great news for you. You do not fall apart when he or she leaves you. You simply move on to the next step in your growth.

One of the biggest problems with your belief in marriage is the fact that you think you are saving you from having to live your own life. You now feel like someone will take half the responsibility for life and you will have less responsibility for you. This leads to great misunderstanding and hurt and resentment when you finally realize that he or she did not save you from living your own life.

Now; on some level you each experience needs and these needs, whether they be conscious or unconscious, are what lead you to another for love and support. When you reach a level where *you* meet and deal with your own needs, you will no longer require others to fill you up with their love. You will function freely from your own love and light energy. You search and search to find a perfect mate because you are searching for God. God is love and love is not what you currently believe it to be.

It is time to explain about death. You do not die, not ever. You are a constant wave that vibrates and oscillates through this universe. Death is simply not possible. When you begin to lose someone that you care for, they actually begin to *move* to a space of non-time. They prepare themselves for life between worlds and go to a space that has been prepared. Even when an unforeseen accident occurs it is planned for. Some part of the body is in charge of the various preparations that must occur.

So far it is not accepted to die. It is feared and you behave badly after death occurs. You are so attached to one another that you begin to fall apart when one spirit chooses to depart. It is not such a bad deal. The one leaving is sent on quite a mission and is often surprised and even pleased to find himself (or herself) out of body. He/she is usually quite euphoric about this death situation. Some even return quite soon after death so they can get on with their education on the earth plane.

You are not to be so afraid of death. It is a door and luckily that door swings both ways. You may enter this plane or you may leave this plane. It really is not too important to God if you wish to stay here or if you want to return. The reason I give you information at this time is simply to calm you down so that love may come *in* to you and you may have peace here and now. It is as in the Our Father prayer, "heaven brought down to earth." So far you are so afraid of dying that this fear is holding you even tighter to this plane or dream. When you can learn to accept all and simply allow all to occur without judgment interfering and saying, "oh, this is terrible," or, "that is awful and horrifying," you will have balance. With balance comes peace of mind, and with peace of mind comes God flowing through your lives.

You do not understand a great deal and yet you make judgment calls on everything that happens in your world. If I can just get you to stop playing judge for a while, then I will have a new role for you. This new role is keeper of the light. Please give up this part that you play and allow all to occur and judge nothing… no right, no wrong. Just love, peace and total acceptance of everything.

Now it is time to begin to show you exactly who you are and stop this dream. You do not always respond well to coming awake. Some of you will take longer than others and some are waking now. It is no surprise to any as to the state of affairs for your civilization. Some of you are very advanced in your technology and others are quite behind in what you would call the race for success. Success is not exactly what you believe it to be. To be successful can mean to have lots of stuff, or a pile of money, or lots of land. Success to the spirit is something else altogether. It is knowledge and wisdom. It is coming out of the darkness and into the light.

The more material possessions you carry, the heavier your trip *up* into the light. You may wish to leave your stuff behind as Christ taught, or you may wish to put it on hold. Have someone else take over the business for awhile so you might learn to un-attach yourself from it. It is okay to work, it is okay to have piles of money and it is okay to love "having." It is just a little more difficult to wake you when you are holding so tightly to the dream. The dream of success and the dream of spiritual awakening are two completely different things. One has to do with accumulation and growth and expansion and the other has to do with letting go and going within and an intake of idea without expansion.

So; most of you hold so tightly to your stuff

because your stuff has become part of your identity. If you would have a hard time driving an old, beat up car because "what would everyone say," or "you wouldn't be caught dead in that thing," then I highly suggest that you let go of this desired identity and go out and rent an old jalopy to drive for awhile. And when you are asked, "What happened to your car?" simply respond that you are changing your image. You no longer wish to be Mr. or Mrs. Big-new-shiny-"rich"-car. Now you want to be different and stand out and see who you really are.

It is not bad to have nice expensive things and it certainly is not bad to 'not' have them. You have begun to believe that it is not good to 'not' have big expensive stuff. I must change this belief, because not only is it not bad, it is quite good to know who you are without the need of identity support such as big titles and shiny new cars. You are so afraid of being a nobody that you began to create an identity based on what you have or what you do for a living. Stop teaching that digging ditches is bad, but selling life insurance is good. It does not matter. Neither one exists and neither one has anything whatsoever to do with who or what you truly are. It is not your true identity. It is simply a role in a dream.

Now, when you begin to understand how you do not exactly *know* much, you will begin, for the first time, to know something. At this time, only in letting go of what you believe will you begin to see who you truly are. You are looking out at the material world through a looking glass. You have a distorted view that says, "Grow stronger and bigger and richer and happiness will follow." This is untrue. Money will definitely follow, but unfortunately money is not God and only God brings happiness.

No religion, as yet, can begin to teach you who you are because religion has lost its way as you have. Listen to your own heart. Do not be led astray by getting deeper into judgment. At this time most religion teaches you to not be sinners by breaking rules that no longer apply. We have moved on in evolution and in awareness, but religion has had a very difficult time with *change* and creating new ways to deal with new situations. Unfortunately, religion is stuck in the past and is very afraid to come into the present. And who or what is religion? It is a belief in some words that were once written from the standpoint of a place in time.

Everything changes. We grow, we learn, we move on. Religion is mostly stuck in time. They want Christ back to do it all over again. This will not be. What will be is a new *view* of God. No more judge with a big book full of names and acts to be punished for. This time God will be viewed as intelligent, wise and accepting, tolerant and loving. No judgment on anything whatsoever and no punishment handed down. Can you handle such a God? Are *you* ready for a non-judging, non-frightening, loyal and loving God? We shall see.

So far it is not God who frightens you so much as it is fear of the punishment God is said to hand down. I have been very patient with you all and I have listened to stories regarding my ways for thousands of your years. Now it is time to set the records straight. Do not continue to believe that I am an intolerant ogre who brings down his wrath on either individuals or your entire planet. You fear me and you hate me for all that you *believe* that I have done to you. I did not! I do not, and I will not. Stop believing lies about God. I go through hell every time one of you believes me to be judge and jury. I go through whatever you create for me by your belief. Stop punishing God by taking on distorted views of him. It is not that you know what you do, it is simply that you don't realize your power yet. You are God and you are punishing your own God for not being loving and faithful to you, when in actuality, you are that very same God who you punish.

It is actually backward, or the opposite of how it appears. God is not light. God is in darkness because you chose to hide God from your own awareness. Allow God to come to the light. Allow God to be seen and known. Allow God out of you by acknowledging that you create this prison for him. Allow him to see the light of day by showing him how you feel. Show God the love you feel for him by forgiving God. Forgive God for what you have judged against God. Forgive God for the sin against you that you believe he has caused. Allow the God in you to move into the light of awareness. Do not keep him suppressed any longer. Give God a break and let him out of jail. He has been misjudged forever.

Now is a good time to begin to teach you about love. Most of you are so afraid to love because you are afraid to lose. Love is acceptance and most of what love does is forgiveness. Love *allows.* Love does not stop or block or deny. Love is God and God *accepts* everything in this creation as part of God. Nothing is outside of God, as God is all that exists. To imply that something is not God is to imply that more exists than God. More does not. God takes up all time and space and thought and creation. So, if it exists, it is in God. If it is not part of God it simply does not exist.

So often you speak of Satan and his power, and you use him to frighten and control others so they might learn to follow your rules. Satan is not separate from God. All energy is *in* God and no one and no thing is outside of God. Satan is fear energy and is very strong at this time. You are taught to fear Satan and what you are fearing is fear energy. You are not so certain he does not exist, so you allow him to be some monster who might attack you at any moment, when in actuality, he is you. He is the fear of God in you.

Now you have done it. Now you have created a double edge sword. Stop fearing God and you lose Satan. How about that? No more Satan to blame for evil and violence. No more Satan to vanquish to the pits of hell. If I were to simply remove Satan from you, you would be lost without his pull to battle. You are so locked-in to fighting for good and destroying evil that you would be quite bored with no evil villain. So, for now I will allow you to keep him.

You choose to believe in a villain, who simply does not exist, out of fear of looking at your own true identity. If you are God and God is Satan as well as all other energy on this level, then who are you? You are the totality of God. You make up the cells that God uses to form his own body. So, if God is composed of all that is, you too are composed of all that is. Stop hating and fearing Satan, you are simply hating and fearing your own fear energy. Stop fearing and hating and judging God, for once again, you are hating and fearing and judging you. An eye for an eye simply means that when you project the thought out it comes right back to you because you are literally all that is.

So far it is most difficult to slow you down. I want to get you to begin to see all differently, and you are so busy spinning out new lies for creation that I must put out fires at every turn. The best way for you to help from where you are is by consent. Give your consent to allow everything to exist and coexist. Stop judging some things as bad and some things as good. When you judge, you create greater separation and at this time I wish to return to you. It is most difficult to return when you are so busy moving further and further from the truth.

Do not be afraid to be who you are. God does not fear God and he does not fear Satan. Energy is simply energy. Some feels good, some does not. I wish you to *change your view* or *perspective* so that all might *flow* and learn to accept. By learning to accept all parts of God you are learning to accept all parts of you. There are no bad guys, there are no battles to be fought. Please do not teach this in your churches. War with Satan is simply Armageddon and Armageddon is simply you *fighting* with you. *There is no one else here.* This battle has gone on for millenniums and I wish it to now end. Leave the Devil alone. Stop killing him and executing him in your mind. He does not exist, but by your belief in him you give him power. You are fighting an illusion. It is not good to make enemies where none exist.

The bible has a great deal to say regarding Satan and I wish you to begin to take these truths with a grain of salt. No one wrote the bible but you. Of course you would use terms that you already believed in. It is not true and correct. It was written to show people how to survive in an age of prophets and psychics who were frightened of the least little thing. They were given words of comfort at that time and now the words have been distorted and misused. Let it go. Let your bible represent an interesting time in your history, but do not *use* it for an excuse to do more fighting, be it with your own self or with your neighbor who does not agree with you. It is simply a book. You scream and shout and push at others to buy this book and it is not even current. It is out of date and yet timeless.

Do not fight for this book. It was never meant to cause battle. Let it go. It is simply words on a page. Stop buying into this trap of fear and deception. You are buying into separation and judgment. God is not the villain he is portrayed to be in areas of this book, so why do you continue to hold so tightly to it? Is it maybe out of fear? Do you fear not having rules? It is okay to have freedom and to trust God with freedom. Don't be so afraid of you that you shut down who you really are. You are in denial of your true identity. You are really all that exists and you do not need to punish you, nor to fight you off, nor to put you down and be afraid of you. You are the light of this world and I do hope you will soon *allow* that truth.

So far we do not begin to see how good life can truly be. You are a multidimensional being and only your focus is in this reality. When I can encourage you to move your focus into a clear view, you will no longer feel fuzzy headed and confused. Confusion is simply a symptom of not being in clear focus. When you begin to see all clearly, you will begin to operate on a new level of awareness.

Most of what I say to you is to show you how you do not have all the answers. You are stuck on a view to the right or to the left. Most of you simply have your own point of view and will not allow anyone else to explain their point of view. You vote and the majority wins. The only problem with this whole process is that stupidity is often rewarded. I am trying to teach you to see *all;* both points of view and everything in between. When you can put yourself in his or her shoes and see from his or her vantage point, you will better know how to allow them to keep their view.

They are not meant to change their point of view unless they are ready to. Scare tactics and brainwashing are not for you to use. Use your own good sense and leave my children to their illusions. You too walk in a dream and if their dream says it is okay to commit suicide *allow* them their dream. It is not your dream. You have your own life and your own dream. If you continue to flow over into his or her dream by controlling his or her actions, you begin to *own* his or her dream, as well as your own. Give it up to its proper owner. One dream is enough for you to handle. I can't get you out of this one, so do not take on another's world.

You are so caught up in right and wrong that you are teaching this lie to others. If you begin to control by telling him (or her) what to do, then you have greater responsibility to bear. Most of you are so full of fear that you control others in order to feel right and smart and knowing. When, in actuality, you are creating clones of you. This is what I meant in our fourth book when I said that you are malfunctioning computers spewing out misinformation.

So far it is very difficult to get you to stay within your own world, or dream. Most of you think you have all the right answers, so you rush at everyone else with *your* truth. I want you to know that your truth is basically all lies and someday you will see how this is so. Basically what I would like you to do is to cop to the truth for a change, and when people ask just say, "I don't know, I don't have the answers to this one," or better yet, caution with, "Well each side has it's view and I think we should just let them each stand on their merit and see how it goes."

Stop trying so hard to prove how right you are. *If* you are so smart, why are you here reading this and trying to make sense of it all? The smartest man alive is he who admits to not knowing all the answers. I know this does not set well in your current situations *within* your material world, but I am raising you to a level of consciousness *above* your material world. Ascension is a time of lifting up and rising above. It is not a time for being stuck in the mud of materialism. Rise above all and come back to knowingness. Accept all and come back to love. Don't you see? If you can teach yourself to accept *everything* exactly as it is, you will be accepting you! And who are you? Love… and God!

Now it is time to discuss sex. So far you are very, very confused about who you are, and sex is a big part of this confusion. You are not simply a sexual being, you are a multidimensional being. This means that sex is connected to everything else. You make love, or have sex with another and this excites the nervous system as well as pumping great amounts of adrenalin through you. You now are in an over excited state and release will come at some point.

So what is this *release* that you experience in climax? Release is passion built up and sloughed off. It is energy built up and released through the adrenals. So far not much research has been done to discover the whys and hows of this process. Mostly it is a calming process. When your body has been overworked or stressed out it is good to release the built up anxiety and stress through sex. It is actually a very good way to become casual and comfortable. It allows you to rest and to enjoy excitement at the same time. Sex is actually a very good game and a wonderful tool to aid your body in recovery from stress and other energy build ups. It is too bad that most are teaching that sex is bad, or nasty. This is not true, but then most of what you teach on planet earth is not true.

So, if you wish to have sex it is highly recommended by God. Violence and sex do not co-exist and I do not wish for this to continue. Rape and sexual abuse are creating greater fear both in you and in those who are raped. It is best to abate all violence. Do not fight and struggle. There are those who are willing and eager to have sex, so do not force your self on those who do not wish sex.

Mostly, I wish to caution about incest and child abuse. Because of the great trauma it creates, it is best to not have sex with your children. You are not wrong to do so, you are simply scarring them for life. They cannot handle the trauma caused by the belief in guilt and you are creating greater guilt for you as well. Until we can get to a point of ascended thinking, without judgment placed on these acts, it is most important to avoid these acts. It will help to diffuse this entire situation if you simply get your sex from those who are consenting and willing. To have sex by coercion, or force, is not helping raise consciousness, it is deepening darkness. It is best to wait until your view point as a planet begins to shift.

Sex is not bad, ever. It is just too powerful for you to handle at this time. And how did sex become too powerful? You gave it power by fearing it, so now we have even greater fear around this simple process of expelling pent-up energy and body fluids. You are so afraid of death that you now attach death to your next greatest fear which is sex. Now we have two power giants hand in hand. Sex does not kill you. You have a virus caused by fear of living and enjoying your bodies. When you become afraid of you, you *create* something to stop you from enjoying you. You created AIDS out of sexual guilt, and I wish you could step out of focus and see through God's eyes to see how silly you are being. But since this is just a dream and soon you will wake up, I will forgo showing you just yet.

It is most important that you begin to calm down and stop screaming and shouting and rushing about to protect your rights and their rights and his rights and her rights. Leave it all alone. Stay calm and begin to meditate. Don't get so *involved* in the drama because you only create more drama. Fighting is not good for you because you are out of touch with the truth and you only fight to say more untruth. Give it up! Let it go! Be love and light not war and demonstration.

It is not such a good idea to excuse yourself from love. Most of you believe that to not love one another means to hate or not get along. In actuality this is true, but it is also so much more. To not love is simply to not accept; to not acknowledge or see. Seeing is the first step to loving. You must first begin to see everything differently, then you will begin to *accept* without judgment. Once acceptance is made, love is there. To see any situation as harmful has a great deal of judgment attached. Once I can get you to see everything through the eyes of love, or acceptance, then you will have peace of mind or the absence of fear. When fear leaves, darkness leaves. You begin to experience life from a whole new perspective or *point of view.* Nothing need ever change in your world to bring you peace. The only change that is necessary is in your own way of seeing. Stop seeing the bad and allow all to be good. Stop showing fear and show acceptance. Let life *flow* in and around you, as it is meant to.

It is not so important to not see who you are, so stop hiding you from you. You actually have the capability to love and accept, you just don't know how to love and accept. Most judgment that you carry is centered around trauma from past life or this life. Trauma tells you to not get involved with, or caught up in this or that situation. Many of you are already beginning to heal by looking at some old memories. This is very good. Most of you carry highly charged energy that is packed with childhood pain. Childhood pain must be accepted. Do not deny your hatred and do not deny your anger and fear. Let it all come to the surface. Healing is what will allow you to see and *accept* all parts of you. You are hating you by cutting off parts of you.

You began to take on trauma as a child and now the trauma you took on is buried deep in you. You saw trauma at every turn. A baby cries and is frightened easily. This creates small pain that magnifies and becomes larger pain. As pain is pushed down, which by the way you still do, it becomes trapped and it begins to grow deep inside of you. As you begin to clear all pain your life will not seem to function so well. Do not be disturbed. This is simply childhood pain coming up and leaving. It is still alive *in* you and for ascension it must find its way to the surface.

Now; not all are ready to clear or raise the dead yet. Raising the dead for ascension is simply raising all parts of you who are trapped and in denial. All must move to acceptance and love. Energy that is blocked is dead energy. And how does dead energy leave you? Through the bowels and outward. So, do your enema and ask God to show you all parts of you. This healing has begun and you will find many who are also healing. Many heal differently, and you will know what is best for you. You will each be guided to accept what you are most capable of accepting. Some are able to accept a great deal more at this time. Acceptance is based on "lack of fear," for without fear there can only be love... acceptance!

Now is a good time to discuss how you wish to see all. Most of you do not want to be angry and hurtful. You have been screaming to see "heaven on earth," and my efforts to show you a new way to view your world are well received by some and totally rejected by others. This, of course, is as it should be. Everything is actually happening right on schedule.

Most of you are so afraid of not being right that you begin to accuse others of being wrong. When you accuse them of being wrong you are actually allowing only your way to exist. When you allow only your way to exist, you cut off others and their creations. Your creation is valid and you readily accept it because you feel its truth from within. Other creations are not valid to you only because you have no feel for them. You do not stand *within* someone else's beliefs, so you begin to deny what they see as their truth. When you deny their truth, you deny them their existence, or belief in their own created reality. Most of you are so afraid of being denied that you actually defend your existence, or believed reality, before anyone even threatens it.

You are very much afraid of being alone so you create a circle of friends who see as you see, and grow and change as you grow and change. Friends are actually a support system that you have created in order to abort your loneliness, and often, to keep you in line with them. If you have someone who agrees with you, you feel best. If someone disagrees you feel unloved, unwanted and unworthy. This is why you argue. You are acting upon emotions and beliefs from childhood that tell you how you are stupid.

As a child most of you felt stupid because everyone was always reprimanding you and scolding you in order to teach you. So now when you are reprimanded, or told your way is no longer valid, you become upset and feel that "your way" is going to be taken from you. What I want you to remember here is change. This is a great time for change and it is growing every day. Let go of your need to be right. You may keep your beliefs, but add new ways of seeing to them. You may keep your fears and insecurities, but add new insight and new ways of seeing how you respond from these fears and insecurities.

It will help you all to know that it is only natural, at this stage in your development, for you to be confused. Don't be alarmed by revolt and don't be alarmed by anger. Don't be afraid of anything that exists and you will find happiness in the center of chaos. It is not necessary to change how a friend treats you, it is only necessary to change how you feel about their treatment. We cannot spend all of our time trying to change all of them, or even convincing all of them how we are seeing things, so give yourself a rest. Stop trying to convince anyone that your way is right or best. Allow all my children to grow at a speed determined by each of them. Do not judge them for their choice of direction and you won't be judged for yours.

So far it is most complicated to live on earth and it is only because you have made it so. You have gotten so wound up in your own creational thought that you are unable to backtrack to see how you got to this line of thinking. You are the most complex because you chose to be, and now you are unwinding you to see exactly how much you have created. In this process of unwinding or unraveling we begin to discard rules; rules that no longer apply and rules no longer needed in our effort to protect us from discovering our true identity. As these rules drop off you will feel free. You will develop new rules for awhile then they too must be discarded. In this process you might begin to feel a little off balance because you are beginning to let go of a specific identity. This identity has been part of you for so long that you feel a little lost and confused without it.

All will come back into balance as you discover how to create once again within your new and less complicated, or rigid, identity. It is not difficult to let go. It is difficult to be torn apart. The letting go is by choice. The tearing apart is by force. Do not tear apart the life, beliefs, ideas, hopes and dreams of others. It is their choice to hold on to their identity as it is. You will have a great deal of trouble just unwinding your own *created* identity. It is not so hard to unwind as you believe. It is just meant to be done in a very gradual process and with a great deal of love or acceptance. Change you but let them be. Don't control, manipulate or harass others about their choices. You are not them, you are you.

So; how do you deal with someone who is trying to change you? You stop them by not stopping them. You allow them to say, do, think their way and when they push their way at you, you may walk away. You need not explain yourself to them and you need not criticize them. You are so programmed to fight for your rights that you teach your children that to run is a crime. "Stand up for what you believe in" and all that. It is okay to run when you do not feel good in any given situation. It is not meant to be *wrong* to run. It is good. Fight or flight is very natural and when you teach your children to stay and tough things out, you are forgetting about abuse.

Abuse exists mostly for those who either don't run or can't run. It is sad to see you believing that you cannot use your most *natural* of defenses, which is to leave, get out, get away because something is not right. When you begin to use your instinct instead of your rules, you will be much happier. It is not wrong to protect your physical, mental or emotional body by getting out of and away from someone who does not have kindness for you. You are most important to God. You love you, and you will be God again. Part of you is very, very natural and it teaches you to "leave when the going gets tough." I wish you well with this new insight.

So far it is best to allow you time to unwind. When I rush you, your pain becomes great and your confusion grows. So, this is what I shall do. We will develop a positive contact with you, and then each evening when you sleep we will converse with you and make certain you do not forget who you are.

It is not so difficult to converse with you when you sleep. You enter a dream world and it is closer to reality than when you are awake. It is not necessary to be in an altered state for God to communicate with you. It is, however, helpful if you are not so strong in your beliefs. God does not wish to cry on your shoulder here, but it would be of great assistance if you could become broad-minded and even open-minded. You are so closed that it is not possible to reach you. You are so busy defending your rights and struggling for more, that you have little or no time for God. God does not require a great deal to get a good foothold in you. He is love and light and to allow love and light into your life would help you immensely.

So far you are so afraid of death and God's wrath that you will not listen to broad-mindedness and enlightenment. Whether you know it or not you each fear God and you each fear the Devil or evil. So; this gives you little solace. Either you fear God/love or you fear Satan/fear. You are stuck in a world that will not allow you to worship as was meant to be. To worship is to love God or accept God. In this world you are taught to fear God by those who separate God from you. You are taught that those who communicate with spirits are evil and even witches or darkness itself. How will you ever come out of these *dark* ages if you do not begin to communicate with God? God is waiting to be born, but everyone is in such a tizzy about how this should or should not be that we may never get to the actual birth.

It is best if you can begin to calm your fears and superstitions by learning to trust God. Let God be love and light. If you believe God to be a monster you will be very hard put to recognize me when I arrive. I have never left you and you have never accepted me since you left. It is not fair to not know your own God-self. It is not right to be afraid of your own voice within. It is no more than superstition to get into fearing your own passage, or journey, within your own consciousness. It is all you. Discover and enjoy. Don't be frightened by the boogie man. There is no evil. It simply does not exist. Let it go. To believe in evil only creates evil. It is not wrong to fear evil, but it will certainly drain you at some point, because you will actually be fearing you.

*I*t is not difficult to become God. The biggest obstacle in your way is fear. You fear loss at every turn. You have become needy and dependent upon the material plane. You need love and security to calm your fears.

Love usually comes in the form of parents, friends and lovers. You even need children for love. This is not bad it is simply misplaced. Every energy must come into balance and move to its proper place. Love must come from you to you. You need not send your love out to a mate in order to receive love. You may simply love yourself directly. This eliminates such great fear when you are abandoned. Love you and depend on God for your security and it will no longer matter if he or she leaves.

It is best if you can, or will, begin to fall in love with yourself soon. You are so afraid of "not having" that you are getting deeper and deeper into holding on to this dream. It is not wrong to want a mate, or lover, or child, or even a pet. It is, however, very difficult to get you to concentrate on loving you when you are so busy trying to milk a dry cow. This is how you appear to God. You push and push to get love and acceptance from another when I am busy teaching the others to love the self first. So; if they are to channel their own love to the self how can they possibly fill your tank? And, why don't *you* fill your own tank with love? Your car runs on energy. Use your own love energy, do not take it from others. A child does not *need* a mothers love or it will die, and you do not *need* another's love or your world will end. It's not necessary to make such a big deal out of the coming together of spirits or the leaving of spirits.

You enter this dimension for your own reasons and you leave for your own reasons. Why on earth would you hold so tightly to someone who is leaving when you did not make his or her spiritual life plan? How can a child grow and develop into a new-thinking form if the child only accepts what you know? What you know is so low on the scale of intelligence within this universe that your vast knowledge is very limited and narrow-minded. You have not the capacity to broaden your own horizons, so step back and allow the new thinkers to see it all differently. They will only *change* what is meant to be changed, and they only reflect your own fears of lack and loss.

You are so afraid of loss and death that a great many spirits, at this time, are volunteering to die (as you call it) just to show you how you fear death. You do not know how fearful you are until your fear buttons are pushed. In seeing, or looking at, or accepting fear, you will change fear to love. It is not so important to show you how frightened you are, as it is to show you how you hold on to your fears and try to project them on others, by convincing others to fear what you fear.

Take *your* abortion issue; fear is so out of control

on both sides, that now we have war in the streets over whether or not a spirit has power over its own material form. You are so afraid of death that you claim the incoming and uninvited spirit, or visitor, has all the power of the adult form. Very interesting twist on creation. Never before have you created this one. Then on the other side, you have those who are so afraid of losing their rights over their own form that they fight for their right to control what is done with it. It is not wrong to abort your unborn child. It is not your place to take on the responsibility of others. It is your place to love you and to bring you back to God. Anything else that you do here is of no importance what so ever. It is all you having a great big dream. I just thought you would like to know.

It is not so long ago that you could not wait to return to God. You began to enjoy matter and its effects on you, but you were not *attached* to this material plane.

As you go along you seem to *need* more and more. At one time it was not necessary to have electricity, but now you would not dream of living without all your appliances and gadgets. This is okay, but it is *becoming* a dependency that is attached to fear of lack. It is good to flow into and out of this material adventure without becoming a part of it. It is as though you become more and more material, and less and less spiritual. You are not your body. Your body is the suit or costume that allows you to exist *in* matter. Do not become a part of matter by becoming dependent on matter. Learn to use and enjoy whatever material wealth you create, but also learn to let go of whatever you create.

This is the cycle of creation. Sometimes you will lose great material wealth or possessions just to show you how you have great fear attached to loss of such fortunes. It is mostly at these times you turn to God and ask why I am punishing you. I am not. For one thing, you created everything, and you took it away also. For another thing, you began creation as a means of flowing in and out of matter, not to get stuck in it, so now you are getting unstuck by creating loss. Lastly, you begin to *feel* fear as you lose and then, and only then, do you realize how great your fear of loss is.

You may walk around this planet (or dream) from now till doomsday and you will boast how brave you are and how you have no fear, but let you begin to *lose* your *hold* on materialism and you truly freak out. You scream and shout and kick and cry, just as a baby who has lost its pacifier. And that is exactly what you are. You are this tiny confused baby who does not understand about growing and evolving, and so at the loss of your pacifier you freak out and kick and scream for it to be returned.

At some point you will grow to realize that you never really *needed* a pacifier for anything other than your own gratification. To suck on something makes you feel loved, just as to suck on the material world makes you feel loved. To pull at a nipple is no different than pulling in material wealth. It is all self-gratification and it is all false relief. So now, to mention to you that "when you grow and leave this dimension, you must leave your pacifier behind because it is not *true* love and security" is most disconcerting for you.

You are so very, very attached to your pacifier. But of course, this too will change. In telling you this, I hope to calm your fears of future *experiences,* whether these experiences be gaining or losing material wealth. It is not important to have. It is not important to not have. It's okay to falsely pacify the self as long as you realize this is simply a pacifier and not the reason for living.

It is not so long ago that you began to learn how to love. You were taught primarily by your parents or those who raised you. And what could two loving parents teach you about love if they themselves did not know love?

It has been a life long job just to *clear* your current definition of love. You each carry your own beliefs concerning love and most of them are based on how you were received by your parents. You believe that love is given when people give to you, because this is how you are programmed. It is not necessarily love when you receive a gift. Often it is those who wish to get closer to you, finding a way to *connect*, so to speak. Mostly it is a Christmas obligation or anniversary, and has absolutely nothing to do with love. It is interesting to note here that some gifts are even given out of fear. The giver may fear losing the love and acceptance of someone, so he or she buys them something to make them think that he or she is truly wonderful and so very loving. This of course is an attempt at bribing, to get attention or love. Often it works for a while, but soon fades when the money or gifts run out.

So, how do you *know* love? It is not a commodity to be bought and sold, and it is not changeable. Love is constant. No matter what occurs you will still love. All of these other emotions are fear. When you must have someone's attention and do not receive it, you get upset. This is wanting nourishment from outside of your own center and I suggest that you come back to you and learn to nourish the self.

It is not so long ago that you did not *need* others for nourishment. You fed your own needs, but now you have such low self-esteem that you attach to another and use their energy to nourish your own *needs*. This is of course a pacifier and a form of sucking on another's energies. This is not love, this is attachment. Let go of all attachments. Do not need to hold onto others for your happiness. Allow everyone to flow. Men and women were never meant to be so addicted to one another. It is not good to be so unloving to the self that you must seek love outside your self.

So; if mom and dad taught you one thing it was to *depend* on others. Of course, how else does a baby survive? But now you are grown and I wish you to turn your dependence from others to your own God-self. Begin to trust that God loves you and begin to love you by loving God. It is not so difficult as you believe. Most of you are so afraid of God that you will not trust him to provide for you in any way whatsoever. It is not wrong to want and need, but it will not bring you to God unless what you are wanting and needing is God.

So far it is most difficult to get through to you. You are not so fearful as you are blank. You are totally unconscious to who and what you are, and you are especially asleep when it comes to the meaning of your existence. You are not so much alive as you are dead. You do not totally exist here on earth. This is but a pinpoint of your total consciousness. This is such a small or minute part of a total picture.

It is not so much that you are not properly focused, but that you misinterpret what you see. This became your primary objective. You began to look around and see *through* matter and it was most intriguing and even disturbing. You could not identify all that you saw and so you began to label your new discoveries. Some you called good, some you called bad. Basically, you had it all. You could play in spirit and control matter as you created. Now your playing has turned to judging and condemning. The things you once created to amuse you, you now judge as harmful.

You created sin to stop you from creating too much fun. You were having such a good time choosing new ways in which to express your creativity, that you decided it was best to stop before you got too out of control. Control seemed to be a very important aspect to your creation. Sort of like creating a monster in a laboratory – you want very badly to create, but you are afraid that you will create bigger, or more than you can handle.

So; in order to keep fear to a minimum, certain rules were decided upon. Hence, we have sin and rules. Anything to keep you under control so that you do not frighten you. And, of course, we all know that the best way to control the other spirits is to put the fear of God in them in order to have things go your way. This way we have guide lines and rules for all to live by and *you* don't have to be frightened about not being able to handle creation.

We have one little snag in all this. The other spirits are no longer believing your rules that you try to enforce on them, and now you are seeing an uprising, fighting, and revolt. It won't be long before everything falls back into balance. You will stop judging and simply allow creation to be without your need to rule supreme. You see; there is only one supreme ruler here and I do not choose to rule, so I gave you free will. So you tell me, what will it be oh mighty Gods of earth? Will you continue to control for fear's sake or will you flow with creation for love? The choice is yours as it always has been.

"*I* am so glad to be alive" is often said. It is so untrue. You do not wish to be alive, because it means death to your spirit. In order to be born you must die. The human form is set up to accommodate only a fraction of what you are. So, to arrive in form is to deny the totality of your spirit. It cannot survive in such a tiny focal point as a human body. This focal point is so minute that it is not in the least bit disturbed by the fact that it has no connection to its owner. It is totally convinced that it is on its own and without contact with its owner. So it is dead to the rest of its body or origins. The funny part of all this is that it is not only a tiny fraction now inhabiting form, it is an absolute. It is tiny and minute but total and complete all at once. This is due to the fact that all spirit exists in every fragmented spirit. There is no energy from the totality that does not carry the truth of the whole or complete energy form.

So, it is necessary here to explain why and how you are dead in order to have life on earth. When this tiny fragment of spirit focuses *into* a body or form it is mostly just looking through it, not actually inhabiting it. Actually, this is most difficult to put into words or pictures. Your brain is a part of you and yet its job is to transfer thought, to break it down and send it through. In much the same way, your spirit is breaking through matter as a thought. It is creating and controlling matter through a process of evaluation or judgment – "yes, this will do, no that won't do." It's sort of like a scientist who is fumbling around in a new suit he created for his experiment and he is deciding as he goes what will work for him and what will not work for him. Spirit is deciding and adjusting situations for you as he goes along creating through you.

The biggest problem in all this is the lack of communication between the body that is being used and the spirit who is driving the body or form. So far it is most important to keep you calm and trusting, because you who read these words are beginning to realize that there is more to this than simply birth, living, and dying. It is not so bad to be you; you are the co-creators in that you begin to create right along with spirit as spirit is the one driving you.

The biggest problem seems to be in your magnetic field. *You stick to everything.* You are so addictive that once spirit begins to move you, you pull everything else along with you. You are stuck on the material plane, or better put *it is stuck on you.* So, when you begin to read and learn new ways of seeing your world, you begin to demagnetize or take off instead of put on. Hence, I gave you the image of peeling layers off an onion. You have become so magnetic that you feel you *need* everyone and everything for your happiness and security. I wish to show you how to lighten your load. Put down your burdens by letting go and trusting God.

This is a very big time for trust and faith. You are taught that the end is coming and that others have all the right or good answers, and you must find your way through all this darkness and fear. Just remember that you have a driver and allow spirit to take over. Body does not trust spirit because body is programmed to believe it needs more to live. It actually needs to de-densify and to lighten its load. It is not always good to climb the highest peak with so much weighing you down. Let go a little and feel the weight of responsibility drop. I know you are being told at this time that to take responsibility is good for you and I want you to know that responsibility is ownership. If you wish to own a lot, be it possessions or people, you get to carry a lot. If you wish to only own you, you carry only you. Your choice has always been your choice. No one can take that away from you.

You must remember love. Love is not addiction to. It is not attachment to. It is not fulfilling one's needs on someone else. It is not insecurity. Love is acceptance of all creation and allowing it to flow. Love does not conquer and show title to. Love gives and is constant.

So, do not be misled by those who tell you that you

must carry more up the mountain. It is not your job. Each individual cell within this entire body of God knows exactly how to save its own self and is designed to do just that. All pieces of God will reach God because they already are God. This journey back to God is a mind trip. You go back by going within and you cannot go back by going within someone else and riding their energy. It is your own trip back *in* your own consciousness to see who you really are. It is all inside of *you*, so I highly suggest that you stop looking out-there for your happiness and for someone to love you. Take a chance and take the trip of your life into your own soul.

It's only a little frightening, but once you get past your biggest judgment against God, you will *trust* enough to go within. Then you will be allowed to see how you do not love you, and this will be the doorway to enter. This doorway, once it is opened, will lead you to self-love. The pain of looking at self-hatred feels very much like hatred. It is the pain that holds you back the most.

Self-hatred is based upon all judgment made against the self for all wrong ever done by the self. This is why I am teaching you to no longer judge. Your pain is so great that it is taking over and controlling all of creation. Everything is made either good or bad in your world of creation and I want to bring you back to the wonder of it all, not the judgment and accusation day. Just look at situations, do not judge them. Allow them to be and you will be holding back judgment on you. You are killing you a little each time you believe you have infringed on someone's rights, or slighted someone else. And I am here to tell you to stop seeing it from this view point of right/wrong, good/bad and see it from love/acceptance, peace/calm.

❧

Now is a very good time to decide how you wish to live. Do you wish to be aware or do you wish to sleep? To sleep is not bad or wrong and to be aware is not bad or wrong. All paths to God work.

So; why all the hoopla about getting back to God and waking up if it doesn't matter? It's your way of *seeing* the total picture. Some of you wish to become more than just a focal point. You wish to know who and what you are. Others are quite content to live in darkness. This is due to the fact that not all parts of God are at the same level of evolution.

As you know, it is most difficult to force a seed to sprout before it is ready. You are each propagating a new line of thinking or a new thought wave. As you begin to take on a new look and new colors you will begin to *feel* these growing or expansion pains. It will be most difficult at times, as you have no sense of what direction your life will take. You are beginning to sprout and this is all new to you. You will begin to grow in stages. First very rapidly, then waiting, then maybe more surging. Each individual cell or seed is arriving in the new age at his or her own rate. So, if you are to allow the others their own choice and rate of growth, it is best not to push at them to catch up to where you *think* you are, or even to grow faster.

Most of you are so caught up in pushing at your own self that you begin to push at others. You feel that you are being worked on to grow and you are. You are literally pushing you *up*. This is all very good and keeps you growing at a good rate. It is however not necessary to push at my other seeds. They are love and light just as you are and they will eventually grow to where they are meant to. When you push at others you simply do not wish to be alone in your awakening process. You are so accustomed to having someone for support because you have no trust and faith in you. When you begin to have trust and faith in you, you will no longer *need* to draw people to you who will tell you how wonderful and right you are.

You are mostly afraid of being alone. You want to be with others in order to receive attention and to be needed or loved. You do not wish to let go of one another. It's like trying to push a new suit of clothes on a giant centipede. You are all stuck to one another, so now we can't get just one pair of pants to fit over all your friends too. Come away from the others long enough to graduate to a new level of thinking and seeing. *They* do not need to see what you see and they do not need to agree with your point of view. Get unstuck for awhile and form your own view point. It is not necessary to debate to convince them.

You just concentrate on knowing what you know and allow them to know what they know.

It is most difficult to teach you when you travel in a pack. All of your friends must agree with you before you feel safe about your choices. It is safe to be you. It is safe to see things from your point of view, and it is safe to be you and to move out on your own. This is growing up and waking up. So; sleep or wake if you wish to wake. To those who wish to wake I welcome you. To those who wish to sleep, "good dreams to you."

So far it is not you who hurts. It is God. God has no way to contact you. You are separated from God by your belief that God is better than you, or more dangerous, or more powerful. It is true that God has memory, but it is also true that you have memory. Open yours. When you begin to remember, you no longer feel so complicated. You will begin to see how many of your memories have a bearing on your choices. In remembering where you have come from you begin to *know* who you are, how the layers formed on you and how to unravel them.

It is most important that you begin to see who you are. How can I get you to *accept* being God if you are not willing to look into your own past and unravel it? Let go of childhood trauma by looking at it and see the direction you chose because of this trauma. A layering is done in one way or another to protect and defend you from life, a layer of hardened thought concentrated around the belief that this or that felt awful, so we must now protect from this or that ever occurring again.

It is so simple to see. If you are creating pain in some area of your life, look and see why or how you create it. Why do you not give to the self? Do you believe that you are not worthy? How did you respond to this teaching? And who knew best for your well being, the one who taught you or your own intuitive self? Let go of the pain and judgment, and the *condition* of your life will change. The condition is often a symptom of something much deeper. If you feel great pain being sick, you have been taught that to be sick is weak or undesirable. After all, being sick is simply clearing toxic waste from within. If you have a problem with your children attacking you verbally or physically, you are attacking you verbally or physically for not loving you. You must begin to see how your reflection is part of your world. Everything within reflects without. If you believe you are a mess you will create or draw messes to you. Clean up you and your mess will leave.

You clean up you by loving you. You love you by not allowing you to judge you. You are not judge and jury so much as you are hangman. You have been mistreating you for so long that you would not know what to do without your pain and abusive self-treatment. When things start going well for you, your subconscious self throws a wrench in the wheel of life to stop your good. Why? Because you taught you to put up walls of defense. You got a little love or hug from mom or dad, but then you got spanked or yelled at. Your voice said to not accept the loves and hugs of life because along with them you must receive pain. So, on earth your true definition of love is attached to pain and abuse.

Now can you see why you all search for love? You never knew the true meaning of love. You thought love meant receiving something that makes you feel good. Love is not receiving hugs and kisses and attention. Love is in you. It comes from you, not from them to you. Love allows you to allow yourself joy, peace, happiness. Love is not *need.* Love is.

Not all has occurred according to your time. You are so into time that you have no sense of space and growth. Most of you are such a minute fraction of the total being, that the total being has forgotten he has you. You are so splintered and fragmented that you do not exist within most dimensions. You are but a speck of dust, a fragment of lint. You do not exist much at all. Your consciousness is focused through a teeny-tiny peep hole and this is what you call life.

You actually have no life. You are like amoebas growing in a test tube only you do not grow that fast. You are stagnant from lack of growth. Your growth is created by stretching, stretching is created through thought, thought is controlled by belief, and belief is what you are. You are the very beliefs that you carry, layer after layer and deposit after deposit of old hardened thought systems that create you. Your beliefs create your identity. If you believe you die then *you* create death. If you believe in God then *you* create God. Not much left to deny now is there? You *are* the *I Am* of *all.* It is all you. Nothing else is here. You may call God intelligent life force, or intelligence, or life force, or energy, or thought or belief, or a big bang. It's all you. Do not hide from who and what you are. You not only create it, you are it.

You depend on others and I want to bring you back to depending on you. You are life force growing into life. You are thought traveling out from life force. You become belief after which the thought created. You are all parts of the whole. You write it, you produce it, you act it out and you *are* it. I am you. You and I are one.

Now; when it comes time to go back to God, how can you if you are already God? You *choose* God. You choose God over life. You decide to be God again. You decide to come back out of consciousness or the true unconsciousness. You are so turned around that you forgot to remind you to not get *into* the picture you were filming. You dove in. You became the focal point instead of the cameraman. Come out of this movie. It's not real. The dream is the illusion. It's only God's imagination at work. Wake up to see the truth. Light is truth. Darkness is not real. Let it go. Let yourself wake up your sleeping God. He is under your spiritual power. He is buried *in* you under your fear and debris. Clean out your body, your mind, and set your spirit free.

You are not supposed to be in pain. You were never meant to be pain. You were never meant to go into matter. It was meant to be enjoyed and simply played with. You have gone too far and become a *part* of it. How? You think it is so, and it becomes so. Un-think it. Open your eyes. Un-create the pain by letting go of judging everything as good or bad/right or wrong. Live in peace and harmony by not arguing and fighting. It doesn't matter who is right, because you are all right. Let each individual cell of God's created body express as they see through their own belief or thought system. Stop turning on people for not accepting you or your way. It is not wrong to not accept you. You hurt because you do not accept you. If you totally accept you, you will have no problem with him or her not accepting you.

You are you. You are not him or her. You are one body with various ways of seeing. All parts of you do not agree at all times – so what? Big deal! Leave the others alone. Stop yelling at them to change. Be you and let them be who they are. If they wish to change they will ask for advice. When the child is ready to drink he will ask for water. Leave them alone until they ask. It is not wrong to give advice. It is just *how* you do it. You are so into power and controlling others that you begin to take over to the extent that you become part of the problem.

Do not push at one another. Let love take care of your need to fulfill yourself. Do not fulfill your needs at the expense of the others. Stop pretending to not care for yourself. Stop putting others before you and stop hating you. When you take the time that is needed to look at your pain, you will begin to heal. Do not force others to heal just because you feel better now that you are healing. Let everyone be.

Now is a good time to decide just how you wish to be born. God of love is being born in matter and his children are going to act as the womb. God will rise up *inside* each of you. He will become so much you that you no longer fear being love and acceptance. He will bring with him peace and contentment, joy and happiness.

For those of you who decide to take part, this will be a most momentous occasion. Most of you will be ready. You will have prepared your bodies and minds, and you will have descended into your own pain and resurfaced again without too great a problem. The road to birth is paved with heartache for some, as heartache is strong on earth. You will see your fears and meet your personal demons, and arrive safe and sound in the lap of God. God will rise up so strong within you that peace will come immediately.

There is no place within you that is safe from exposure to God's light. You will open and *receive* God. You will praise your own God-self and allow those who open to the light to praise God as well. You will have *arrived* through billions of minute fragments that once were created for housing the spirit. The temple of God will become the seat of God's love. You will arrive at first in small doses of light and continue to emerge *through* matter as is allowed. You will shift the consciousness from fear to love and know only peace.

This process is not difficult, but it has its downside. Its downside is the clearing of matter to speed up your vibration. This clearing takes some time and patience on your part. You first begin to realize that you are not perfect and then you begin to let go of your need to be right. Once you have let go and let God take care of right or wrong judgment, you will create an opening for love or light to enter. When light enters it makes no sound and no visual change in your features.

Light has a very rapid vibration and as you take on more and more light, you will begin to see more and more pain. This also shows itself as confusion. It is natural to *become* in chaos. Chaos is your origin and when you go back and unravel your pain and fears, it will seem as though your life is turning around and becoming a living hell. This is due to the raise in vibration necessary to bring your fears to the surface. As long as your fears are buried *in* you, I cannot enter. Fear is dense. Light is light.

Light does not necessarily enter you. It is actually in you, but can only operate in the absence of darkness. So much darkness is here at this moment, that to turn *up* your light would blow you up. You have vibrated at such a low speed for so long that to begin to speed your spin would throw you out into space with no way of retrieving you.

So; I wait patiently for each of you to ask to be lifted up, for each of you to want to be saved from fear. It is not such a long time ago that you began to ask. It is not such a long time ago that I began to speed up this process. It is not so long now as you believe. You are getting stronger by letting go everyday. Each time you let go of how you *believe* things should be, you give God power, your own God-self.

Now, most of you believe it is best to let no one interfere with the teachings of religion. I say "let it all go." None of it was taught in the manner which you now perceive it. You create greater fear by preaching fear of God and judgment by God. A few historians put pen to paper and meant well by this. In the same way that some will misinterpret what is written in this series of books, you will misinterpret what was taught thousands of years ago by someone out of another age. It is just not important to read these teachings and pass them on. It is no more important than teaching business methods that are out of date. It worked for a time, but things have changed and technology provides new ways of seeing who and what you are.

When you join together in prayer, it is best to pray for love not forgiveness. When you pray for forgiveness you are creating more judgment by suggesting that you were judged by God. You were not, are not, and will *never* be judged by God. You must let go of this belief system in order to *receive* God in you. Your own point of light is not allowed out of your depths because fear and judgment lay over it. Let it out by peeling away fear and judgment. The light of God is at the core of you. You are God and you reside deep in you. You must un-layer the cover that stops your light from shining. Take it off. Peel away fear and belief in judgment until your light is shiny bright.

*I*t is most important to begin to discover your true identity. You have begun the process by which you will awaken and you must not forget to be you. You forget to be you by not being 'all accepting' of every occurrence with which you become involved. It is best to not involve yourself with too much at this time, mostly to keep you from creating greater fear of your journey within. You become a little tired or cranky or exhausted and it frightens you. You believe you are getting ill or stressed and you struggle to maintain your energy level. It is most important for you to rest and to stay calm. You are being separated in order to *heal* you. You are not seeing as the majority sees because you are being reprogrammed in order to clean up your attitude. You are being cleared of past beliefs and judgment. This is a very big step in getting you clear. You are just one out of many cells who must clear. It is most important to allow all to clear at their own rate. Some are jet airliners and others are slow sailing vessels. It is not important to push at yourself or at them. Allow all to occur as it is meant to.

Mostly I wish you to know that you are not alone. There are those who clear at great speed and great confusion, as well as pain. It is these who will take the lead as they have attained the light and left the fear.

Now; it is not required that you suffer in order to reach God. This is a big myth. It has been taught that those who suffer the greatest have God's ear. The pain and suffering have to do with how much judgment you have always placed on yourself. And since you do not even know your unconscious self, not to mention your many other bodies, how in the world can you know how much pain and suffering you carry? It is best to get it all out. Allow pain to leave in whatever way works for you. Allow yourself to lay down and escape your daily chores if it becomes necessary. To push at you when you are clearing and releasing is most stressful for you. Let you be. Let your body and mind heal by clearing your psychological debris. It is not painful to leave it behind. It is painful if you must hold on to it. It will eventually kill you.

When you see someone who is going through

childhood or past life do not stop them. Allow them their journey within. If they acquire pain it is old pain leaving. You do not *create* new pain to come into the light, however you may *feel* and re-experience the old hurts as you see where you came from and how you got to be you. So; do not believe that God asks you to suffer, but know that you chose to re-experience in order to let go of your pain and fear. You chose because you wish to go faster to the light. Take your time or speed it up. The pain *will* come up to the surface either way. Fast or slow, it does not matter. Some are ready now, others wish to wait. You choose.

It is not so long ago that you began to discover who you are by counting your fingers and toes. Much in the same way that a baby discovers all of his parts you have been discovering yours.

You discovered your sense of decency and, oh, how you loved that one. To be respected and admired became a top priority for you. You began to like to stand out, to achieve what others could not. Pride rose to great heights and your self-esteem slowly, very, very slowly began to fall. As you began to achieve, you began to see the differences between you. You are not yet able to let go of your desire to achieve better and better, so I will ask you to simply slow down on this area for now. You see, to achieve is not wrong, it is just blown all out of proportion. It has to do with gain, *material* gain. So, I ask you to reconsider your views on holding to the material plane at this time. To desire the material world holds you to the material world. To desire God holds you to God.

Now; when you began to admire others for how much they have achieved in this material plane you began to show yourself how you did not do as well. So now your subconscious does not believe you to be as good as these high achievers. If you have no material possessions how much easier is it going to be to let go of this material plane and go to God? Do you see how things in this world are important *only* here and not on any other level?

The rules you have created for this plane are definitely not applied in any other area of creation.. In all of creation money means nothing. Only here in this dream does it mean anything and only because you made it one of your top priorities. Only on this level of creation does it mean anything to learn to read or write and that also is because you say so. Elsewhere in creation it is *known* who you are and how you are still babies on the scale of evolution. This is not to put you down this is simply to put you in perspective. You are not advanced compared to the rest of creation; you are quite behind and quite slow to learn. So, now I have offended you and hurt your feelings. *It is not wrong to be last!* You have this very big judgment against being the last guy in the race.

Actually the last guy in the race may have the

easiest time of it. All the others have experienced the run, so the track is smooth and well worn. The energy of earlier runners is able to guide the slower runners in the right direction. So, don't be hurt to know you are last. After all, you only use (at this time) a very small portion of your brain.

Why do you think you do not use full capabilities? Maybe you have a plan for creating heaven on earth, and maybe if you used full capacity of your brain, you would develop more rapidly and not be in place for the birth of God. Maybe all that you do really has a very good reason. Maybe you should stop judging one another for not being winners, when you are all winners just by your presence *in* matter. Maybe the others didn't wish to go to earth or the material plane, because of all the hazards of getting back out! Maybe you are actually a very brave soul and don't even realize it. Maybe your mission is actually to bring the light into the darkest area of creation. Maybe you are all channels for the light of God and are allowing God to penetrate a new area of creation. Maybe you work for God and you do not remember that you do. Maybe you got stuck in matter and are now signaling God that your mission has become most taxing, and so God is now answering your call and telling you to stay calm while I work on getting you out of this dense realm.

In order to bring light in I must appear at some point in time and space. Light is me and I am you. Turn on! Remember who you are and why you came. Love. Love. Love. Acceptance will get you back home to you.

You desire heaven on earth and you *are* the light.

It is not such a good idea to just sit and complain about your life and its problems. Most of you do not wish to change and yet you do wish it (life) would change for you. The way to create change is in your attitude. When you can learn to *see* all differently, you will begin to experience great change. This change will be physical as well as emotional and psychological. It will come when you have gotten out all the old stubborn programming that believes you are hurt. You are not hurt and you have never been hurt. Your belief in pain comes from this pattern of fear. Whatever you fear is what you become. You began to fear and mistrust pain and now you *hold* pain instead of letting it go. It works like this. Pain is a signal. Pain says, "Don't put your hand in that fire again or it will burn up." Pain says, "Don't wear that belt so tight as it pinches and bruises your skin." Pain says, "Do not jump off the roof again for you will break your leg."

Now; without pain to signal you, you could jump and break a leg, but you would not *know* you broke something, and it would not get the rest and care it needs for recovery. Pain warns you not to step out dancing just yet, because the broken bone is still tender. Without pain to signal you, you would run and dance and fall very quickly with a re-break of the same bone. No healing would occur without the doctor saying, "Stay off this leg." Pain was created to act as a doctor. You could jump from an airplane and break everything in you without knowing, if pain did not tell you.

So, what went wrong with pain? How did you get so full of hurt? Your pain began to rise to a level of screaming because you began to ignore pain. Your "will" began to take over and tell you, you didn't need to listen to pain. You could not afford to rest and act like a baby about a broken limb, so you decided to walk whether there was pain or not. The more you created stress on the broken leg the more you felt you were overcoming pain and learning to tell pain how you did not need to listen to him. He did not care, because his instincts told him to do this job of creating feelings of hurt, in order to protect various parts of the body from gross negligence. He began to send stronger signals just to get through to you and you began to ignore him even more. He eventually gave up on getting your attention, but he never gave up his job of sending the signals.

So now you still ignore his signals and force yourself to keep going for the sake of money or whatever, but it is not your job so much that keeps you from listening to pain when he signals you, it is your fear. Fear of surgery, fear of death, fear of healing, fear of not having. I can understand fear of surgery, as it entails cutting away at you, and you fear losing more of you. But to fear not having a job to return to because you have been out sick (or better put, "out healing") is very, very weird, don't you think?

How many of you are afraid to quit your jobs because you believe there will never be another good job for you? How many of you hate what you do? How many of you are just plain scared to death of not having? Not having is a very big fear. Why? Because you are addicted to this material plane and to matter. Have, have, have, more, more, more. I say let it all go and it will begin to *move.* It is *stuck* from your hold on it. Let it move and let it go to return in a better way.

All energy is meant to flow. Pain will even leave to return in a better form. Everything is energy. Everything is free floating and can move if you allow it to. Stop stopping life and stop fearing letting go. Allow life to flow and move. Do not hold on or you suffocate what you hold on to. You are not meant to be stagnant. You are meant to move, to flow, to love by acceptance and to change earth to heaven. How can you possibly see heaven on earth if you will not let go of your *idea* of what earth must be? *Let it go!*

It is most important that you begin to see who you are. You are not so dull and boring as you believe. Most of you do not begin to understand the meaning of your existence. You are but a flash in the existence of time, but you think you are time. You are a spark that flashes on and off. You vibrate, or oscillate back and forth between here and God. You know, yet you deny. You see, yet you are blind. You are one giant being who is projected through many tiny cells and now you believe you *are* only each individual cell because each individual cell sees only from its own view point. So far there are billions and billions of cells but only one being of light. So, who is the light? Is he the total being? How are you so sure you are 'not' God if you are so sure you are here? How do you know who and what you are and how do you come out of this coma you are in?

So far you have not the ability to believe who you are, so it will do no good to explain. When you empty your programmed ideas of what is or is not, you will begin to have space and energy for more and greater information. Until that time, I must work with you from the standpoint of what your current beliefs are. It is only from where you are that I can lead you out of this illusion. So, where are you and how did you get to this point? You came in on a beam of light and you are that beam of light. You entered *into* a very dense area of space and time. Time does not really exist, but in order to teach you I must deal within the bounds of *your* created limitations. One of the reasons you are so *stuck* in your thought flow is that you traveled deep into space and met darkness head on. Darkness appears to be dark nothingness, when in actuality, it is heavy and dense. It appears dark as it is built up energy.

Now; when you began to enter this darkness you were affected by it. *You changed* from light to dark. You began to take *on* this entire dark realm in order to enter. You also could no longer *see* who you were, because you are no longer how you once were. Hence, we have time. You were this, now you are that. You were here, now you are there. Time was created simply to explain away all the bad choices you *thought* you made. You decided to go into darkness to change darkness. Your choice is not bad. You are alive and kicking. We must now get you to change back to the light, and all darkness will lighten also. It is a very good plan and it is still in the process of *becoming*. You only need to *remember* in order to complete your plan.

So, when you wake up enough of your own cells, you will enter the light of your own beingness, and oh, what a beautiful day that will be for all of creation. Bring you back to the light of your own beginning. Love is light. Light is achieved through peace, and peace is achieved through acceptance of all occurring. Do not waste your time planning for some big blast. This is it right now. You enter your own consciousness and change your own viewpoint. The Second Coming is just that simple and the change from dark to light is just that subtle. No big fireworks display, no big choir of angels singing and weeping, just little ol' you *becoming* little ol' God.

So far it is not good to scold you. You are so afraid of God that when I tell you how you are stuck you become frightened. You have been unable to see your way for some time. Mostly you have been in a maze. You are trapped by your inability to see over the walls. You are so stuck in your own fear that you do not wish to hear how to get unstuck. You are afraid that you will create further pain by getting further information. You may begin to feel uncomfortable or just not ready to know more. This is natural for your level of fear. You will become more and more receptive as you begin to realize how tangled up you are. You are so multilayered that you do not even look like you. You have created vast amounts of stringy goo that covers you in a big ball of string. Mucus is not so bad as it is sticky and undesirable from the standpoint of being free. You are all tied up in this sticky, gooey mess. This mess of course is within, as all is within, and at some point you will begin to unravel your "gooed" up thinking.

Now; as I have explained throughout this series of books, the way back to you is by un-layering and peeling away until there is only you (the true you) left. The process by which you may unwind and unravel is enema. This method is highly recommended by God for getting you back to you. When you enema, you may begin to actually see these old layers come out. The mucus will begin to dissolve and retreat in the process of enema. Most of you still have a great deal to learn about the care and cleansing of the human form, but since you use so little of your brain, you can understand how unknowledgeable you are. Yes, they may laugh at you for doing enema, so I suggest you keep it to yourself. It is not wrong to care for and clean out you, but superstition is very strong among you and fear of anything that you do not understand is great.

And how can you understand your own body when no one has the courtesy nor the knowledge to teach you? Your parts are referred to as private or unmentionable, so how can you possibly begin to enjoy and love a body? You can't even mention the parts in public. So until this obsession and "fear of your own bodies" changes, I suggest you keep your business of cleaning your body to yourself. It is so fearful on earth at this time, that some of you are very confused and believe you have *rights* over the body of another. If you wish to tell another how to treat his or her body without his or her invitation to do so, you are way out of control. Actually you are so *into* controlling that you wish to live the life of another for them. Get your own life in order and leave everyone else to theirs.

You are not meant to be in pain and conflict and you are not meant to be *in* someone else's life. You are getting all tangled up and I can't unwind you. Come back to you. Live and let live. You have your own life and your own reason for being here. Stay in you. Do not project into the life of another by running their life in any way. Stay put, stay calm, see God.

So far we do not know how to save all of you. You are so stuck in matter that you appear to be drowning or suffocating. You cannot begin to see your way out, so you create your own return.

Most of you are so full of pain and anguish that you resist any kind of salvation. The reason you do not wish to be saved is your projected belief in judgment. Once you begin to stop judging others, I can get you to look at how you judge you. You may have pain left over from childhood or you may have self-resentment because someone led you to believe you were bad. Mostly you all have pain. Your society teaches good and bad, so you all know or believe yourself to be in the wrong in some area. With childhood trauma the belief in judgment creates a belief in punishment. So, if you were told as a child to be quiet because the adults were present and speaking, you now believe that adults have power, or simply rights, over you. So, if you do not *agree* with adults or those in authority at this time, you judge you and punish you depending on how severely you were taught this rule.

So now you are an adult and every time you do not agree with politicians or government or police or a boss, you are breaking a rule that was taught to you as a child, and because the child *remembers* being punished for talking back to authority, you will find some way to punish you for talking back to authority. Many of you have very low self-esteem and a very difficult time with confrontation. You are not weak, you are being punished and are tired. Tired and sick, not weak and spineless as you believe. Most of you are so afraid of more punishment that you fight back with guns and knives and defensive attitudes. *You are not afraid of them, you are afraid of you.* You punish you because you were *taught* that right is right and wrong is bad, and you are not good if you do bad. So; your psyche will find a way to sabotage all the good that you wish to create for yourself, because it was *taught* to do so. Constant programming of a belief will *create* the belief in living color.

"Perfect example"… Put the fear of God into people and enough people will *create* flood and famine and disease. Stop believing what you believe. Give God a chance to show you a way out of your own created illusion. I am here to bring heaven to earth. It is not so difficult as you believe. Let go of *all* past programming that says you must be punished. I did not create rules for you to live by, you did. I did not punish you for your sins, you did. Stop punishing you, by allowing peace. Stop punishing God, by allowing him *free* reign. Stop being so afraid of doing what you want. Let everyone do what they want and all will come back to God.

Stop being so afraid of your own shadow. You are killing you from the inside out because you believe you must control your evil side. You have no evil side. You carry anger and hatred because you are angry at your own self for all the pain and judgment you carry against you. Let it go. Let God in. Return to the light of truth. I have given you the means by which you might begin to discharge old programming. Use it. Do not continue to fear your own self. You are so vast and so dense that you are fighting with you right inside of you. The war is not in the streets of your cities. The war is right inside of you and it has raged forever. *You* have an opportunity to see God, to go to the light of understanding and leave the pain and ugly lies behind. Be bold enough to see through your fear into the light. Be bold enough to see the truth and come out of your darkness. Be bold enough to set you free.

It has not been easy to tell you who you are. For one thing, I must be *received* before I can be heard. In this particular case, my pen has had the opportunity to either reject me or allow me to be. She has been most cooperative in many ways. To inhabit form is a very complicated task. It is perceived, at this time, to be a great gift. Mostly it is part of this process of becoming God.

When my pen first agreed to do God's work, she had vague to no idea how I would *use* her. I have used her as one might use an experimental rat or guinea pig. It is not often that God is given permission to completely take over and reign as he sees fit. This, of course, has to do with free will and your choices. Most of you refuse to suffer more than necessary, but you still suffer without your awareness of this suffering. In the case of my pen, she was told little and asked to trust. She has cleared a great deal of pain and now understands on many levels how you can unwind and remove the dense layers. She has gone into her pain and re-experienced her childhood trauma and now she is free. She has not been such a bad case as she believes.

Now; if you do not wish to see your pain and release your pain, you will be permitted to keep it. But then why would you want to? Addiction maybe, or just *fear* of re-experiencing it in order to free it. It is not attached to you, you know? *You* are attached to it. It will not be difficult to begin to see how you have judged, just ask. Ask often and you will begin to remember. As you begin to remember, you will feel the hurt and trauma and ugliness that you created as a child to hurt you for doing your awful acts.

So far, none of you is exempt. You all grew up with rules of good vs. bad, so you all have pain of punishment for breaking your rules. Some of you have created very elaborate ways of hurting yourself for not being good. You take away things or lose them. As a child you were punished by losing play time with friends or maybe just losing television privileges. So now your psyche will remember and punish you by losing that part you so desperately wanted in a play, or simply losing your favorite necklace or watch. Either way it is all you taking from you.

Now, as I begin to show you how your psyche works, I do not wish you to create more friction between you by causing more judgment against him. Your psyche *is* you. He is your own programmed mind. He does nothing without your consent and he follows your rules that you created. So; as you begin to clear your psyche programming, I wish you to stay calm and *allow* everything that is lost to be lost. Don't hold on, just let it all go because it is not important. Do not create greater judgment and pain. Know that I am teaching you and you are simply learning to let go and let God handle this situation.

When you can begin to not fear loss you have begun to not fear gain. Loss and gain are one in the same. One is movement of energy and the other is movement of energy. Let it flow. Let it go. Let it move. Creation is meant to flow with you and around you and even within you. It is all going according to plan so don't get afraid and block the plan simply because you do not understand it. There is very little that you are capable of understanding and I highly suggest that you turn yourself and your life over to a much higher intelligence.

It won't take long to disarm you and get you to peace. You are loaded and ready to fire at anyone who even suggests that you should let go of something, even if that something is pain. You are so afraid of your pain that you keep it hidden and you do not wish to look at it. Only now it is bubbling to the surface in the form of angry explosions, and you will see it reflected in others all around you and even in the Mother Earth, as she releases and lets go of her pain.

Remember, *all energy is meant to move.* It flows and ebbs, don't block it let it go. You will pick up more in the next wave, do not block this wave. There will be another wave, and another, and another. You are so focused on this one wave of energy that you cannot see all the abundance waiting in many other forms. It is not good to wait and not receive. You are not receiving because you do not know gold when you see it. Not everything of value fits into your wallet or purse. You will begin to see prosperity when you tune in enough to recognize it. Do not give so much power to money. It will change and even leave at some point. It is simply a unit of energy. Use the energy that comes to you in whatever form it arrives.

I know that money can help relieve suffering and hunger, but it will not solve your problems, as they are mental and psychological. I am here to lead you to truth, and truth includes all forms of prosperity, not just money. You must get well in order to see how vast your garden is, so that you might partake of all your fruits. Do not focus on one source or you create loss. Focus on all possibilities. You may live like a king or queen and you must still face your fears. Those without money *believe* they are miserable without it and those with money believe they are miserable because they have it. Do not make money the villain and do not make money your God. Let God be God and let money be matter. It is not meant to buy and sell the spirit of man.

It is not time to raise your level of thinking. It will be some time before you are prepared to see above your own horizon. Most of you are so afraid of time and space, and all that exists there, that it is most difficult to allow you a peek. You are totally engrossed with being right and making "right" choices and decisions for yourself.

It has not been that long ago that you worshiped wind and fire and ate raw meat. You were tribal and even sacrificed to your Gods, or God, so as to protect you from his wrath. Only now do you see how foolish and superstitious you were. I will take you beyond your ability to understand and show you how you still make sacrifices to God and you still are superstitious regarding your beliefs around him. His teachings have been misconstrued and even changed. You study a book that was written by men who were even more superstitious than yourselves and you call it the "good" book, versus the bad books I am sure.

Anyway, you are so afraid to speak in vain about what is written in this book that you actually "fear" it. You walk from door to door and sell your good book and its teachings, and if others do not wish to buy you push at them to convince them how "right" your belief or your religion is. I wish those of you who are being pushed at (to buy religion) to simply say "no thank you" and get on about your lives. You do not need what you do not want and you do not need more fear and intimidation against God.

I am not picking on the "good" book. I am simply not endorsing it. I do not wish my children to *believe* that God smites you down for not being good. I am not a convict who you can neatly sentence to live behind the gates of heaven, and I am not the executioner I am made out to be. I am love. Keep the teachings about love, peace, forgiveness, happiness, joy and trust. Let go of everything else. If there is a threat behind it, it did not come from God. This is very simple to understand and I hope you get it. Do not take God's name in vain by suggesting that God kills or maims or punishes. This is a lie and I wish only the truth to be known.

So now I wish to explain for you how you might become God. You will reach into the light by leaving the darkness. Darkness is a state of mind. You are dreaming and you don't like what you are seeing, so wake up to the real world.

When you retire for bed, you actually come closer to reality than when you are walking around shopping and eating and working. Embrace sleep and learn how to use it to awaken to the truth. If you begin to program yourself to dream as you sleep, you may remember some of what you do when you are out of body. Many of you travel and explore outside your body when you are in bed sleeping. This is similar to what your soul has done. It came to earth to excursion and travel. Most of you are actually awake when you sleep. By this, I mean that you remember who you are and you work on getting the attention of the rest of you. You send signals and messages to the central system, but most information is ignored or distorted through the layers built up within you.

So, this has been the system for some time now. We show you how to view the world correctly when you are asleep in your bed and you wake up and say, "Oh, I had a bad dream," or, "Oh, what a great night," depending on how you received your information. Part of you will judge it and part of you will love knowing, just as part of you will judge what I write and part of you will shout, "Hallelujah, we're getting there." So, when you dream in bed it is good to know that you are entering a realm of reality that is actually more real than your daily lives. It's a bridge, so to speak, between the conscious and the unconscious.

I wish to explain this at this time, because some of you may begin to feel the need for more and more sleep and rest. This is a sign of communicating between the conscious and the unconscious. You will also learn that to sleep relieves stress and tension. This is because you rejuvenate to a certain degree while you sleep. Rest is very good and sleep is best. Do not judge you for sleeping and getting in touch with the rest of you.

⁂

*I*t is not so long ago that you began to take on form and duplicate form. You began to see all through the eyes of an investigator. You even saw your fall as very interesting. You saw how you could be whole and yet be a fragmentation. You could focus in and out of form and this pleased you a great deal. You still focus in and out of form only now you do not realize that you do. You are so busy flashing back and forth, at times, that you forget to be whole. You think you are in or out, when you are both. You forget you are God and human when you are both. You begin to adjust by allowing both to be. If you shut off to one aspect of your beingness it does not alter that aspect. You continue to exist and grow in that one area, but you are ignorant to the fact that there is growth. That is, you are ignorant to the growth of this aspect of your own beingness until this aspect walks up and says, "Hi, I am you."

It's sort of like having a baby and not having the ability to know you are pregnant. No one has told you and no one else has ever had a baby. So now you have this kicking inside of you and you know something is going on and, in some cases, you even feel awful. What is going on is birth. The birth of God is coming to matter and no one knows because they shut off and forgot about this aspect of themselves. It is not long ago that you began to reproduce through pregnancy and it will not be long before you are all reproducing and allowing God in. It is not such a big deal as you believe. You simply ask for God to enter you and he will. He does not break down doors. He goes where he is invited and he asks only that you become love and let go of fear. "Big request," you say? Yes, from your point of view I guess it feels that way. But I have a much greater perspective on all things and I assure you that this birth is not as painful as you believe.

The pain is leaving with the entry of God. Pain leaves when God enters. Pain is not meant to inhabit form. Pain was simply a warning system that you began to ignore. What you believe you hold as your pain is not really pain, it is illusion. The pain may feel great, but it does not exist. It is a trick to keep you in fear. It will be a short time before you are capable of understanding pain, but I thought you would like to know the truth.

You will be very grateful (at some point) that you released and looked at everything that you call painful. Pain, as all trauma, is in the eye of the beholder and in the response to his judgment, and even degree of judgment. All pain supersedes all love. Love does not ride well in a vehicle full of pain. Let go of your pain. Get all horror and awfulness and ugliness out of you by not judging things or situations as horrible, awful, ugly or painful. You create your own pain by judging your own world. Try to see the gift in every situation. You are not being punished you are being loved.

How many of you remember situations where you were fired from a job or kicked out of your home, and you landed in a much better job or nicer home? Now, I realize that to you nice equals money. Let go of money and let nicer be more peaceful, pleasant, easier to care for. Just as a better job can actually be one with less money and less responsibility. You are actually getting a gift of greater peace and calm with less stress, and you get upset because you can't see the gift. You don't *know* gold when you see it!

So far it is not you who have failed. It is not true that the human race is not up to standard. What is true is your *perception* that you are not good enough.

Most of you are so afraid of doing the wrong thing that you begin to shut down. How can you possibly do wrong when there is no wrong way to *become* God? It is not simply your fear of doing wrong that holds you back; it is also your need to be right so you won't be punished for your wrong. I want you to begin to *allow* all to occur. Do not block wrong and do not block right. Allow what is, to be what is. When you begin to see how it does not matter you will finally be free.

Most of you have been looking for a way to prove your rightness or goodness since birth. No one wants to be wrong, because punishment comes with being wrong. This is how you have taught yourselves to punish. You take aim at evil and fire, only there is no evil. You are afraid that if everyone is left to their own devices, there will be even more danger. The truth is that those who are suppressed and controlled will always fight back out of a natural need of freedom. Every soul is free, and in some way *knows* that it is. Do not continue to control and break the natural spirit of another. Allow them to be and they will find their own right place.

The greatest problem is that you have each been controlled to the extent that you no longer honor the differences between you, and you are looking for ways to make everyone more alike, or the same. Enjoy your differences and *allow* them to express as they see fit. You will find that a spirit, who is shouting because he is being told he may not shout, will only shout all the louder in order to prove that he is in control of his own existence. *You do not own one another.* You live and love and create, you do not own. Stop putting up boundaries for others to live by. They will all live their lives according to *their* life plan if you stop controlling creation. If you teach one another to not do this and avoid that, you are blocking growth and spiritual cessation is occurring. Do not block the flow of energy. God does not wish to frighten you further, but you all know that a screaming child will eventually stop once he gets all his screaming over and done with.

So; now I have opened a new bag of worms. How do you *allow* a child to express his screams? You take him to a place where he is *allowed* to scream. Just as you teach a child to use a bathroom or toilet, you teach a child to use his own emotional power. Set aside a room (padded if necessary) and allow him to scream away. Always ask if he wants to scream once he begins, and of course make arrangements for his next possible session. If a room is not convenient use the forest or out of doors. It will not be long before he knows that you know he can scream, and I'm certain he will tire of trying to prove it to you, as well as himself.

A child does not scream for attention as you believe. A child screams because he believes he is in pain. He releases in his scream. How often have you felt better after raising your voice? Someone dies who is close to you, and you usually scream when you are told. Do you scream for attention? No! You scream from pain. A child feels restricted in a body because he knows he is actually free floating essence. Now he is on earth and everyone is telling him everything that is untrue to his true nature. Most of what is taught on earth has little, if anything, to do with your spirit. I am here to teach your spirit how to operate *in* matter. You have never been taught the *spirits point of view.*

Now it is time for me to remind you that my pen is just an instrument and I am just her boss.

*N*ow it is so important to not push at you. You are in a state of great change and you are learning to return to your natural instinct. It is not wrong to be in charge of your own life by letting others be in charge of theirs. It is best to allow all to simply be, because you do not know what is best for them.

You are in a position of denial. You do not accept that you are God and do no wrong, so it is impossible to expect you to accept that your neighbor is God and can do no wrong. How will I ever bring you out of judgment of right and wrong? Rules were a big mistake. I thought you might be bright enough in your light to realize that a rule was simply a *choice* for *you*, not something to be forced on your neighbor. You do not need rules. As I explained in our earlier books, I gave you the Ten Commandments out of love not out of a need to control my children. If a child comes to you and he is hurting himself by climbing the tree in your back yard, you too might say, "Don't climb the tree." It, of course, is said in the moment and for his age and ability to comprehend at this time. It is not important and nothing is meant by it except to help the child. Why would he then run to all his friends and say, "It is written, do not climb trees."

So much has been learned and taught that must be unlearned and untaught. Most of you are so afraid of the spirit world that you believe they are all out to harm you.

Funny thing is – *you are they*. If you believe that they are out to get you, you believe that you are out to get you, because you are spirit in matter. Possession is so frightening to you because you view too much television and believe it, and of course when enough people believe it, it will appear somewhere in creation. So; why don't you stick to believing only in peace and pleasantness? Most of you could use a great deal of inner peace and it will come from love and acceptance of all parts of you. If you believe in evil demons you are creating evil in your world. If you believe there is an unknown part of you who may act up from time to time out of a need to be acknowledged, then you are creating greater wisdom and acceptance of who you are.

Most of you are so afraid of ghosts and goblins that you would never consider answering a voice who came to you from an unknown source. It is most difficult to get through, and once I do get through it is most difficult getting your trust. You see; no one trusts anymore. No one believes in miracles unless they cure someone of a disease and no one *really* wants God to break the sound barrier. Why? Because the strongest *belief* in this dimension is that God kills. God takes lives, turns people to stone and floods the earth because he has so much anger and loathing for you that he wishes to zap you at every turn.

God does not wish you dead. God does not care if you are punished for climbing a tree and God does not care whether or not you climb trees or you tear one another apart. It is simply not important in the scheme of creation. The only thing of any importance is *knowing* that you are God, not maybe you'll be someone great someday, but knowing now that you are God. And how can I teach you to embrace being God when you are so caught up in the illusion, that you judge God as dangerous?

Do you see how difficult it is to get through the ignorance and bring in the truth? No one wants to hear the truth because everyone has been taught to accept the lie. You ask why you hurt and I am here to tell you that you are killing you, not by guns and knives, but by fear. The guns and knives cannot harm you. You simply go out and come back in, in a new suit. The beliefs can destroy light. You are very dense and sinking deeper and deeper. Raise your level of thinking. Change your thoughts. Stop controlling others out of fear. Let fear come into the light by acknowledging that absolutely everything is good; no bad, no wrong… just good or God!

For now I wish you to be at peace. Know who you are and walk alone. It will not be necessary for you to travel in packs. You have spent a great deal of time creating relationships and I wish you to know that you will know yourself best by interacting with others. You may sit in your room or move to the mountains, but you get to know you best by looking at those around you.

You are a sum total of all the parts that you see. You each act out different parts to allow yourself the greatest knowledge of yourself. If you believe yourself to be in a position of harm I suggest that you leave. Now; harm and abuse come in many forms and if you do not wish to be treated less than you desire I suggest you move to a better situation. You have all been taught to ground yourself and to put down roots. It is time to fly. Do not be unkind, but do be fair to yourself. Do not stay for them, stay for you. I want you to learn to do for you and not to put you last. You are so programmed to love everyone else before you love you, that I may never get you off the ground.

It is not only okay to love yourself; it is okay to make decisions based on your own well being. It is not wrong to pack up and move when no one else wants you to. To move is your choice and you must take responsibility for your choices. However, if you continue to live your life for others you will never discover your own wants and needs. I know this will not sit well with many, but the true nature of beingness is to float free. What you think of as family ties are just that, ties. You do not lose your family ties by moving. You lose nothing by going your own way, if you choose. You do, however, enable yourself the freedom of choice. If you are in a family who is not supporting and loving I wish you to move, leave. Some of you are already so abused and mistreated that you may never regain self-love. The longer you stay in a psychological situation that has turned abusive the greater your pain will be.

Now; I must tell you something that you are not ready to hear, nor are you prepared to change it, yet. You do not belong to one another, as you seem to think you do. You *use* a body to enter this world and because you use this body to enter you believe you must do whatever the identity behind this body says. You are not answerable to the form who allowed you to enter this dimension anymore than you are answerable to someone who holds open a door for you. You do not owe one another for your life. These arrangements were all taken care of long before your history began, and you cannot owe when the agreement was an exchange. So; do not put your parent or your child *before* yourself. You all suffer pain and one is not more important than the other. Your rules regarding *owing* and *repayment* are not true and correct. No one on earth owes anyone anything. God creates and God allows.

It is not such a good idea to continue to use the words good or bad. You are so afraid of being bad that you do not trust me when I say, "This is not so good." I use your language and I can only reach you through your language. So; in order to show you how to leave the darkness and rise up into the light I must show reference.

Hence, I am stuck with your language.

Did you know that language was created out of a need to communicate to one another after the fall? No one could use intellect to communicate once you began working with rules. You needed a common way in which you express your needs and your pain. You wanted to let go of telepathy because with telepathy you could not lie. You only thought and it was known to others. When you thought in a certain fashion, the others would set you straight. So gradually you began to communicate with verbal noises to enhance your ability to have separate thoughts and hopefully expand at a much faster rate.

Verbally transmitting your thoughts became quite a challenge and most of you began to enjoy the freedom of not knowing what the others were thinking. You actually began to *use* words to camouflage your true feelings and intent. Hence, we had a great rise of false identity, and last minute efforts to save a falling entity.

So far most of you are so confused by your own definition or translation of what something means to you personally, that you no longer communicate. You speak – someone listens, and someone else sees what he wants to see and hears what he *believes* you are saying. Example: If a child has been taught that love is beauty, then he believes that hate is ugly. If he finds his own appearance less than beautiful, he knows from this simple teaching that he is not love (beauty), he is hate (ugly). So; stop and think! What are you teaching by teaching good and bad, beautiful and ugly?

It is not in your best interest to be so unhappy. I must change this area of creation. I know you don't always know that you are unhappy, and at times you even save face by saying you are happy when you're not. The least little thing can destroy your peace. If someone hits you, you feel upset. If someone hits your car, you go through the roof and if someone puts you down, you are sullen and hurt.

You are not so afraid of being put down as you are afraid of being discovered. Here's how it goes. You don't like you. You feel that you are stupid, inadequate, immoral and even ugly. *You* do not know that you feel this way about you. So; when someone hits your car, you feel another ugly stain on your record. You may tell yourself that you are simply upset about the cost of fixing said dent, or the fact that your insurance may go up. However, if you have a choice (which you do) you will fix the dent because you do not wish to drive around in a car that is not attractive. Stop and think before you get angry at the insurance companies; what you are really angry at is you for *letting* this happen. So; do not blame them for the cost when *you* made your choice to fix it at such a price instead of driving it with a big dent.

Today I wish to discuss your health and well being. None of you is in a great deal of love, joy, happiness or peace right now. I wish you to change. Change how you see all that occurs in your life by changing how you see it. If you get hit by a truck on your way across the street, I want you to not judge you for this. It is not your fault; it is only your creation. Do not place blame or you turn it into something bad or wrong. What if there is a miracle in you being hit by this truck, and some part of you created it to show you how you are God? Maybe you will experience an out of body lesson, maybe you will simply die and see the light or maybe you will end up crippled and learn to walk again. You do not need to run yourself down in order to see how you are God. You are protected in a manner that will prepare you to receive who you are.

So; if you get hit and stay calm and watch for whatever will come of this, you have displaced fear and terror and anxiety and pain. What good does that do? You will then have a more than likely chance at healing yourself. All energy is meant to flow, and if you start blocking with judgment the minute you are struck down, you will create pain for you. You are the one who must live inside of you and to accuse others of wrong doing, or even to accuse yourself of being in the wrong will only create greater fear and pain within form. Wrong is made to be a bad thing or a judgment call. So; let it be just something that happened and you will carry less pain.

Are you concerned with getting even or getting restitution or even revenge? This will also program you to believe it was wrong or a bad thing. The greater judgment you place on the wrongness of this event, the greater pain *you* will inflict on you. Why? Because you create absolutely all that *you* see. So you then become your own villain. No; you don't *realize* that this is what you do, but this is truth, not fairy tales about how you were wronged.

So; now we have you afraid of you, because you don't know when you may want to create such an incident. I suggest you begin to love you, then you won't feel the need to punish you for doing what you believe to be bad things. Let it all go, do not judge yourself for winning and do not judge yourself for losing. Silly statement isn't it? Not one of you would judge yourself for winning, would you? Why? Because you have all been taught that to win, or have it all is best and to be a loser is to be last in line.

Well, I see that I have a very big job ahead of me. To lose life is to soar as a spirit, and to lose matter is to gain light, and to be God is to let go of and *lose* everything that you now hold dear or cherish. God is not *gained* through prayer. God is gained through the desire to be God, just as humanity has been gained through the desire to be human and see through human eyes. This is quite an adventure I will take you on. You will only need to *change* how you *see* all that you currently *believe.*

*I*t has been a very long journey for you into darkness. The agreement was to return at a specific time. The time has come. You left in order to find a new *view* point which would allow you to see who you are. God became so involved in expansion that you were literally pushed into position. You were projected out of God, only you went in not out. This is all very difficult to explain to you, because it is not logical nor intellectual from where you are.

You are beginning a new phase of understanding, and this new phase will become your intuitive ability to perceive information. You will receive such information with your right brain and you will pass it through your right lobe for processing. This type of reception will be received differently than intellectual logic. This information will not need proof. You will begin to learn how to arrive at conclusions by feeling and learning through experience. Most experience will bring you whatever you require in order to put you in your proper place for ascension.

Ascension is not necessarily rising up off the ground as Jesus did after three days of death. Ascension is also rising up in your own sphere or orbit. You each contain a private world that is all yours and you will rise above your own world, or worldly thinking. It is not necessary to go anywhere. You may simply change your channel – tune in to a higher frequency. When I suggest how you must let go of *all* and desire only God, it is to show you what you value most. You will wish to value light nothingness in order to have it all. You may continue to hold on to matter until you decide you want God. This is your choice as it always has been. Only those who desire God see God. If you desire the material plane you will continue to play in matter.

Your process of development and growth will depend upon your ability to let go. You hold on to a great deal. The greatest *hold,* other than possessions, is your hold on your belief that your way of handling things is best. You are locked in to your way and will not be flexible. I do hope you will stop pushing to have things your way, when you know how often I have said "There are as many ways as there are ideas." So; if you are one of those who constantly pushes at others to get them to do things your way, I wish you to stop. Stop trying to change your mother or your father. Let them be. Stop trying to change your sister or brother, let them be. It is not your place to change others. It is not your right to live there lives.

My pen has another favorite saying that is popular right now. I believe it goes like this, "get a life!" It's brief but I believe it says it all. Get your own life together and stay in it, so I know where to find you for ascension. Stop projecting into everyone else's business. Stay home in your own life where you belong. You cannot fix anyone else's life when yours is in turmoil. Get yourself together before you set out to teach anyone else how it is. You are teaching lies based on your own fear driven ideas. Keep your belief to yourself until *your* belief is fear free. It's just that simple. Stay out of their lives or you spread your fears to them.

It is not such a long time ago that you were soul. You came here to learn to grow. You began to expand and grow and then you went into your own expanded idea. You began by allowing all parts of you to flow through each idea until idea took on your personality. Your personality began to grow and grow until you could see how you were not alone. You began to see and *feel* other consciousness and this led you to believe that you were not the only one here.

This other consciousness was actually the start of separation and the belief that you are not all connected to God. You are all God and you all feel hurt to be away from God. Your pain is in the loss of part of you. You feel that you lost a part of you and now you wish to regain your missing piece. This piece has never left and is actually the totality of what you really are. You are so afraid of not having you that you create other you's to make up for this initial loss; a fake you, you might say or a more loveable you who is in character for your personal liking. This of course is according to your newly developed personality's liking.

So far the new you has done an excellent job of imitating love, and of course by now you all know that to love is not the issue. Love is. It exists at all times. So, "to love" is a false statement in the first place. It is actually placing claim to, or wanting for your *own*, or placing a great deal of emotional energy towards. This is *not* love. Love is. It simply sits. It is projected no where and you receive it *from* no one. *You are it.* It is you. You exist in it. It is God, you exist in God; God is you.

Now; I don't expect you to love and see love right this moment. You are in so much pain and confusion that your needs exceed your own love light. You believe you must satisfy your needs in order to be happy and actually you *are* happy, only your programming is so strong it prevents you from seeing your joy. What we must do is uncover your joy, dig you out so you see differently in order to know how *you* work. You will see love by looking in a mirror. If that does not do it for you, you need help digging out.

If you believe you must receive love in order to be loved you are mistaken. No one can love you. You *are* love and no one can give you light when you are light. You need not suck off one another to feel whole. You are not loving one another as you believe. You are playing a game and soon you will learn the truth. I do not wish to hurt you and I do not wish you to freak out, but you are about to change *how* you see all, even love.

Love is not "wanting someone and getting them." That is fishing and catching. Love is not "feeling good toward someone because they just helped you to feel better or gave you a lot of money," that is gratitude. Love is not "staying with the same mate for fifty years and enjoying every minute of it," that is loyalty. You do not yet know love.

How long do you believe it will be until you see the light and know God? It is now. It is at hand and you are feeling the change and growth now. You may feel it emotionally or you may begin to experience physical sensations. It is all coming into reality as you know it. The fourth dimension is oh so gently moving into position right on top of your third dimension. You will be ready to receive higher intelligence soon. You will begin to know who you are and you will begin to allow others to be who they are. Soon you will release all fear of not being in control and you will soar with the white dove of peace.

You are moving into a glorious time on this plane and you will wish to know that you do not lose, you only win. Every loss in the third dimension is a foot hold gained in the fourth. You are not in a good position at this time to see how wonderful your new world will be. It is created already and waiting for you. Tune in! Stay tuned to peace by letting go and giving up. You have been taught not to give up and to hold on at all costs. Now is the time to rise above old thought patterns and let the old slip away to the bottom of creation. You are on a joyous ride and if you release enough old buried energy and let go of old ways of seeing, you will float freely into the light of wisdom.

It is not as long as you believe. I have successfully worked with Liane now for nearly six years. She has not learned a great deal so much as she has learned who she was and how she got so unhappy and hurt. As you recall, she invited God to take over her life because she was not happy. She did not know how she was slowly killing herself as a means of punishing herself for past sins. She believed herself guilty of great sins, both from past life and, of course, from her abusive childhood. You don't know how you have hurt yourselves with pain and guilt and I wish to free you all. It is not your fault! You did nothing wrong! You were *never* bad! Not ever! Stop blaming you and punishing you. You did not commit a crime, you simply are God.

*I*t is most common for you to believe that you are

bad. After all, you have been taught that practically every body function is disgusting and since you are your body, that would translate to *you* being disgusting. How can a bodily function be wrong? It cannot. You use your body in order to experience life in this dimension and if you do not allow it to function properly it will simply quit working all together.

From the time you were a baby you were *taught* not to mess your pants. Your parent scolded you when you did or maybe even assumed an air of great disgust when they had to clean up your dirty diaper. You are no more unconscious as a baby than you are now. As a matter of fact, some of you still retain some semblance of the *real* truth as you are still close to your incarnation. So; when you mess your diapers and the one who changes you is disgusted by the smell and the mess, you now pick up signals that you are a disgusting human. You repulsed them by your stinky mess. How can this baby know? We all know on some level. We pick up signals. This is how you decide what is good or bad, what will make you happy or sad. It is programmed into you, and your body stores these truths into its cellular library.

Now you are an adult and your truths are killing you. You believe yourself to be very disgusting and we will clear this cellular programming in order to raise your vibration. Do your enema and allow yourself to discharge the heavy burden you carry. You were never meant to carry burden. Your job is to carry joy. You are the light of this world. How can anything you do be *judged* as disgusting?

You are seeing through false truths. Take off the sun glasses that stop you from seeing the light. You will not go blind if you begin to play with the truth. Let the truth be your friend. You are not so bad as you believe. Deprogram by seeing how you are God.

You will not wish to be afraid of your body. Do not be afraid to touch it and do not be afraid to look at it. Discover you, all of you. Your body is like your car. Know it, love it, keep it clean and running smoothly. You are not disgusting for having a body, so please do not insist how it may be dangerous to show your children nudity. Nudity is natural not nasty.

So now you see how it is almost impossible to push you into the light. You each believe whatever you were taught. You believe what was shown to you through your own childhood experiences as well as other lives you have taken on.

Now; other lives are tricky. Some of you have seen many past lives and others have seen none. Past lives exist only if you have a karmic debt to settle or you are in parallel territory. Most of you do not believe in karma consciously, but you do unconsciously. You have all been taught that you reap what you sow in some fashion. I do not wish you to go *into* your past lives so much as I wish you to re-experience trauma brought forward. This trauma may be connected to an abuse or killing experienced in a parallel universe. You must remember that time, as you see it here, is not correct as it does not exist elsewhere. Of course, you all know that you don't exist either.

So; how do you experience pain and trauma if you are not here? God had a thought! You too may *experience* thought. Close your eyes and imagine a very big car crash and you run up to this car crash and you see who is in this crash. You drag a body from one car and run to the other. Just as you get to the other car you see a form that is familiar to you. It is your mother or your spouse or your child. You choose for this dream, but make it someone you have a great deal of attachment for. Now; as you remove this body from the second car you cry and hold him or her close to your heart. They are dead, gone; you will never see them again. Now how do you feel? Do you feel the pain, sorrow, loss? Was it real or was it *your* imagination? "God's imagination" works in much the same way, think it, feel it, experience the thrill of created emotions.

This is all very, very difficult to explain to you in your terms as your terms are so very limited. You can only see as far as you can stretch your vision and you can only imagine within that stretched vision. You *are* thought; imagination is you. You are parallel to you in that you have many other thoughts and some of them affect you very strongly.

So; know that you can be *more* than who you are

and know that you have no end for you are a thought wave that is moving out and beginning to return. Like a wave on the ocean that rolls into shore. Each wave looks separate as it crashes against the shore line, but then it is pulled back into the whole of the ocean. Who are you if you are a wave of thought that rolled out to the shore and is now being pulled back in? Are you the wave or are you the ocean of thought that this thought wave was projected *forward* from? This is your *thought* for today!

*N*o one has the ability to change on their own. Everyone is required to seek assistance from God. So; this is why you believe so strongly that you must repent in order to receive salvation; you must ask God to forgive your sins and you will be free to enter heaven. How do you ask God to forgive your sins? You ask you (God) to forgive you. You are afraid of being God so you create confusion to keep you from seeing how you are God. You are not *part* of the whole; you *are* the whole as well as the individual. You are all that there is and you *create* all that you see by accepting or denying.

If you don't wish to see something you simply stay in denial. If you do wish to see you simply accept. Now; most of what you see is created out of a false belief in right or wrong. Your rules apply to everyone only if everyone *accepts* them as theirs. No one is allowed to believe more than one belief system because they each contradict one another in certain areas. So; how does one become acceptable to all if one cannot accept all? Most of you are so intent on being correct that you push everyone else to be *your* style of correct. Of course, everyone else already believes in their own correctness, so they don't follow *your* rules for being correct.

Now; as long as someone is correct, someone is wrong. If you have right answers you create wrong answers. There is no wrong way to become God, there is simply God and growth. No wrong way means no right way. I wish you to stop teaching right and wrong. You know how this will be most difficult for those who believe in only one way to God, but you will keep this little insight to yourself for now. No wrong and no right. No rules to live by.

So; how do you raise your children without rules? Here is a good way to start. Use options. Give your child options similar to this. Instead of the rule being so strict about homework time being directly after school, suggest that your child play first for an hour, or watch his favorite educational program, or even eat a good healthy snack. Then ask which option he prefers for the day. You will be surprised at the change in a child when he is allowed to make his own choices within a given selection. Your child will begin to feel self-worth and less controlled and suppressed. He will gain a new sense of himself as well as a new trust for life.

Any living being who is constantly repressed and manipulated will know how to break away from control eventually. Once a repressed child breaks free he will experiment without much restraint. You have cities full of painful, hurt, repressed children who are *fighting* for their freedom. Freedom from what you ask? Freedom from their oppressor. And who controlled and ruled over them so righteously with all the rules and right ways of living? The parent who was simply doing what he/she thought best for a loving child.

I must begin to teach you how to love instead of train your children. It is acceptance that will give you freedom, and denial will give you prison. So, begin to love by allowing. You train each person you love to be you and follow your rules, let them be God and follow God's rule which is love, acceptance, allowing. So far you have not much to learn about life, but you have *everything* to accept. Come out of denial and *allow* everything to be. Allow you to be growing and learning, just as your children are growing and learning. Stop judging yourself for not following the rules that you have chosen for you to follow. God will not punish you. Only your ego self is into punishment. Do not nail yourself to an invisible cross, because what you believe is what you get and if you believe in punishment you will eventually get punished. Stop this nonsense and teach only love. It is not important to follow the rules. It has nothing to do with becoming God.

Originally you needed rules because you were spirit

entering matter and the deeper into matter you sunk the more *human* you became. Now you are becoming spirit while still in matter, and this will allow you to raise matter up with spirit. You will not leave what you have come from. You take all parts of you with you. You will each be allowed to be free of this third dimension by accepting fourth dimensional thinking. It is not long now. Plant the seed and wait. All seeds grow up eventually. Some faster than others. You will all wish to know that every rule you ever followed did have a purpose. Now is the time to change, let go of and fly.

No rules are required for spirit. Spirit simply is and is not subjected to your three dimensional hold on gravity. Your rules for gravity holding you down no longer apply. We are moving *up* and out of this dimension simply by *seeing* all differently. No more denial; accept, allow, be.

So far we have discussed much that will assist you in letting go of your current belief system. It is good to know that you are doing what you choose and not what another has chosen for you. When you get pushy with another about how they operate, I wish you to remember how you feel when someone pushes their ways at you and insists that your ways are all wrong. It is not your job to change them; it is your job to change you. You are God. In changing you, you literally change all because you are *all*.

Now I wish to discuss your right to be alone. You each have a need or desire to be alone at times and this is most important. In being alone you communicate only with you and *your* needs. This is actually a form of nourishment. You heal and grow when you are alone. You do not receive stimulation and excitement from outside of you and you rarely *need* to be alone for long. If you find a need to exclude yourself from family and friends you may begin to look within. It is quite possible that you do not trust people. Usually, not trusting people (or life) is connected to something discovered in childhood. Possibly you got hurt by some family member, possibly you don't agree with how you were treated by people as a child, or possibly you carry deep suppressed memory of abuse.

Look at how you relate to the world and life as it is presented to you. Do you always wish to get high, or drunk, or fight? It is abusive behavior that comes from a background of abuse. Do not be afraid to look at who you are. Start searching for your answers to relieve your pain. If you need help, go get hypnotized. Eventually your subconscious will give up its secret. I tell you this to assist you. Do not be afraid of your own mind and what it contains.

My pen simply asked what to look at under hypnosis and I suggested years five through twelve. She did not realize that she would see sexual abuse and she was smart enough to record her session. She then went home and began to think about what she was told by her own self under hypnosis, and by the end of the week she believed none of it. Luckily she had the common sense to play the recording and *listen* to her own subconscious screaming for help. She was in total denial within one week after her hypnosis. Why? Because she broke her shield of protection.

Loss of childhood memory is very, very common. It is the psychic protection provided by your own mind. It will keep you safe from your own punishment. You believe you deserve to be punished for your sins, and to have a sexual experience as a child is very sinful in your own eyes, so the punishment according to you must be severe. You dish it out like it is a sentence that will save you from something. Punishment will save you from nothing. Punishment will only beat you up and put you lower in your own low self-image. Let go of judgment against you for *anything* you have ever done. We all know in this class how there are no rules, and death is no big deal, and sex is no more important than dancing.

How will I ever be able to save you from yourselves if you refuse to agree to forgive and change? You must forgive yourself for what came naturally in the process of becoming God. It all came naturally as it was all done on the moment or instant with no planning. Even the planned parts are planned long before you thought of them. It's not your job to judge what goes on here. Let go of judgment and you will see peace. There really is no trauma if you do not create trauma out of something as simple and natural as sex. Stop playing in the world of pain. Come into peace and joy. Let God be your creator and let all of creation be a gift.

Now; when you begin to receive memory regarding childhood trauma you will re-experience those emotions just as though you are now experiencing the pain. In actuality, you are experiencing the pain as you release it, or let it go from the neat little cubby hole you had it tucked into inside of your mind. And since your mind is in all of you, you now have this big sin tucked into all parts of you; and as you suffer for your sins, your body will begin to break down and die from judgment against it for doing this bad thing, and from punishment against it for doing it. So now you are slowly killing you and before long your liver or heart will give out from the stress of keeping you going, when you (the inner self) has been commanded by your own desire for punishment to knock you off, and get rid of all the bad thoughts, deeds, and no longer *allow* you to do anything to break the rules of decorum set for you by you.

So now we have you killing you, and you crying about disease because you don't know *why* you are sick and out of control, or maybe just angry at the world. I will tell you now, you are angry at you more than you are angry at them. Stop hating you by looking at you. Look at who you are. Love who you are. Look in the mirror. Love what you see. Stop judging you to death. What you dislike about you consciously is only the tip of the ice berg. Go within and see who you are. If you do not wish to channel your own information as my pen does, then I highly suggest a hypnotherapist who will simply *ask* your subconscious to spill the beans. Ask to know what you are judging you for. What did you do that was so awful?

Have your therapist or hypnotherapist tell you (when you are under or in altered states) that you are now ending your cycle of abusive behavior and you need help from the subconscious you. Go into your childhood if necessary and speak to your child again. Ask for the twelve year old or six year old to be heard. If you have blocked out entire years, those would be good places to start. Get to your pain before it devours you. Stop this process of death by disease now. There is no need to be sick. You are God not evil. Give up on killing you in an attempt to keep you humble and less than God. God is you, you are God. You know it and it is now time to teach your subconscious self to accept God.

Stop denying your good. Allow all to be. Look at all parts of you. You need not spend great amounts of money. My pen was hypnotized once then began to channel all her own information. You too may channel. Anyone can. Receive your own information regarding your own psyche. It's all right there inside of you. Know you and you will no longer be afraid of you. If you have great concern in opening your mind, you can bet you are afraid of you; so when you don't trust people and protect yourself from others getting too close, you are actually protecting yourself from you. You don't want to get too close to who you are. Why? Because you judge you. Why? Because of ignorance and a lot of rules that you no longer wish to follow. Let go, let God and stop punishing God.

Now I want you to find peace. I wish you to look within your own mind and find a place where love is safe. You are so afraid of not having love that you push love aside. You try so very hard to get those you care for to love you only because you do not love you.

When you begin to change you will begin to see how you are indeed lovable. It is most difficult at this time as you are too busy proving to everyone how wonderful and desirable you are. You are not so wonderful that you can neglect you. You are not so desirable that you can walk right into God's arms. Why? Because you put up a wall to keep you away from God. You put up blocks to keep love out because you believe love to be dangerous. Don't you see? Love God. God is you. You are blocking God/love/you/acceptability. Stop blocking love and you will *receive* love. Stop selling yourself short and you will know happiness. You were never meant to have pain; you were created to experience God/love. Be you by accepting and loving. Don't be afraid to love. Allow everyone to know who they are by allowing you to know who you are. You were never meant to be blocked from who you are.

Now is the time to go within and get to know you. Love you and you love God. Hide from you and you hide from God. You are ashamed, so you hide. You created out of fear and now you wish to hide from God. You cannot hide your private parts from God. I wish to *look* at you, all of you. Do not try to cover up. This hiding has gone on too long. No one is meant to suffer. Take off your mask and come out of hiding. You cannot hide from God when God is who you are. *Know you.* In the knowing, you will see how you create all that harms you. You will begin to see how you function.

You will never know you without desire to attain God. You are so trapped in matter that you believe yourselves to be the exact opposite of who you are. You *are* light. You do not sin ever. You do not serve a raging God who is sitting on his throne waiting for you to die, so he can tell you how bad you have been and sentence you to some fiery pit. This is not God, this is monstrous. Why would a God of love create children of free will and then give them rules to never break? It's ridiculous. This whole fairy tale has you in a very big bind.

Now, I suggest each one of you begin to take a good look at how you truly *view* God, not just this you, but the child you were and still are. The programming is so very strong on this plane that it affects you all. Jesus was a man, just like you. Jesus had programming just like you and Jesus made mistakes in his assumptions; just like you. You *are* the son of God. You are the begotten child of God. You are no more perfect or less perfect than the other children. You are all one, in that you are each part of the whole. You create life and you destroy life. Change how you create and destroy, and you change how God creates and destroys.

You are not meant to be the lowest life on this plane. You *are* meant to be, and know that you are, the most glorious. How will I ever get you to let go of judgment? It is such a very heavy cross to bear and it is weighing you down. Nothing is ever bad or wrong. It is not wrong to die, it is not wrong to live. Be acceptable to others by accepting you for all that you do. You all search for love and acceptance, and what you truly search for is self-love, self-recognition, and self-preservation. Save you from the ax. You are killing you for being bad, and every time that you judge another for being wrong you will create an ax to fall on someone, and that someone just may be you. Revenge is a very tricky game. If you play this game, you will reap what you sow. Please do not play this revenge game; it is not what you truly want.

You want to love, you do not want to maim and you want peace, you do not want war. Stop and look at the mechanics of what you do and how you create. If you chop off someone else's head to punish them it is simply a reflection of how you are chopping off your own head to punish you.

So now I have you all worried about chaos. You just can't imagine a world without guns, and law, and rules, and regulations. This will show you how far *you* are from ascension. Those who can *envision* will create their world of peace and harmony sooner than those who cannot. Those who cannot imagine such love with no conditions will be better prepared after this *thought* catches on.

No one on earth will be left out or left behind. You all go, so it makes no difference when. You will each attain paradise as paradise is the natural state of God. So, do not be afraid to *see* all differently. Know you and you will know how you think. If you know *how* you think, you will then be in a position to change how you think. If you change how you think, you change thought or your own image of how it should be. Think of it and it eventually becomes reality. You are at a turning point in creation. You are concerned for yourselves. You are concerned for planet earth and you are concerned for life. Do not be concerned. Focus your attention on allowing everything to simply be and you will see the most wonderful changes taking place.

Know you and you will know how to change the entire concept of this dimension. *You are this dimension.* You *are* all that you can see, envision, imagine – it is all you. You create life, you take life. You create birth, you create death. You give, you get. You are therefore I Am. I Am therefore you are. Do not be so afraid to be God. To know God is to know you. Ask it, mean it and it is yours.

You have so very far to go and yet you are right

here on the edge ready to jump off and fly. Know that your world, as you know it now, does not explode into a billion particles, nor does it disappear from existence. It simply *evolves* into something much, much better. You will see your fourth dimension by moving from fear to love and you will see God by being love. And what is love? Love is *unconditional*, no rules, no judgment, no pain, no punishment. Just allowing what *is* to be what is. You are all so caught up in the rightness and wrongness of your existence, that I must be very patient with you as I wait for you to "just imagine" the perfect world. Just imagine a world without judgment. There will be no anger without pain. There will be no pain when punishment ends and there will be no punishment for sins when judgment is gone. It begins and ends with judgment, and this imbalance of love must find God just as you must find God.

Now; here is a secret to finding God. Look at you. Look into you and you will find all. I am the source of your life and I am the thought behind your search for love. When you yearn for love and peace and joy, you are remembering God and how it is to be God. Your memory becomes stronger as you allow your "desire to reach God" to become all that it can. This is how Liane *created* this series of books. Her memory of love, peace and happiness led to a great *desire* to feel and experience God's love. She reached out to me and I reached from deep inside of her. We now have this connection, and through this connection she may reach her own *desired* goal of heaven on earth. She does not write for you, she writes for God and for herself.

She feels she is learning and *experiencing* each book she channels and she is. She is you. You too will reach out to God in your own way and you too will begin to heal and know love.

You have come very far in your minds since we began this series of books, and you have now completed your eighth grade studies and I salute you. You have done very well to swallow this big pill, but this will begin to heal the wounds that *bind* you to this third dimensional dense level. You will be happy to know that it does not end here. Liane has agreed to write my next book titled, *Forever God.*

I will not give up on you and, as long as Liane is willing, I will channel this information. She is totally committed to me and she allows me to use her time and her body. You too will begin to see the wisdom in turning your time and your body over to you for your own discovery purposes. Most of you have a great deal to see in regards to who you are and how you respond to who you are. In our next book, *Forever God,* we will discuss how you create heaven right here on earth. For now I will say good day, good health and God speed back to you.

God's Pen

I first heard the voice of God in 1988. I was sitting in my back yard reading a book when this big booming voice interrupted with, "I am God and I will not come to you by any other name." I felt like the voice was everywhere – inside of me as well as in the sky around me. I was so frightened that I ran in my bedroom to hide.

This was not the first time that I heard voices. I had been communicating with my own spirit guide or soul for about a year. I guess my depth of fear regarding God, and all that he represented to me at the time, was just too much.

I spent two days trying to avoid the voice of God, which was patiently waiting for me to respond. By the second day I was exhausted from lack of sleep and decided to give in and talk with him. This turned out to be the greatest gift and best decision of my life.

The first book, *God Spoke through Me to Tell You to Speak to Him*, shows my evolution from communicating with my soul to communicating with the Big Guy. It took a couple years for me to be comfortable communicating with God. My fear of a punishing God was big! That has most definitely changed and I now think of God as my partner and best friend.

In the beginning the voice of God would wake me in the middle of the night and tell me it was time to write. He said I had promised to do this work (I assumed he was talking about the soul/spirit me). I would drag myself up to a sitting position and watch in amazement as my hand flew across the page, while I tried to keep up by reading what was being written.

It was always so much fun to wake up the next morning and grab my notebook to see what God had written during the night. After some time the voice stopped waking me and I became comfortable picking up my pen and writing for God first thing in the morning. I think in the beginning I had to be awakened while still semi-conscious from sleep so I wouldn't object too much to the information that was being channeled through me.

As I grew less and less afraid (and more trusting) of God, he was able to communicate greater information. Some of the information is quit controversial, but I felt it important to just let it be and not censor it. I present the writings here to you as they were given to me. I have edited a little (mostly the more personal information regarding myself) and I have used a pen name for privacy reasons. I asked God for a good pen name and he guided me to Liane which (I was told) in Hebrew means "God has answered."

At one point I became a little concerned about my sanity in all this, so I went to a hypnotherapist to find out what I was doing. Under hypnosis I saw this incredibly huge beam of light with a voice coming from within it. It was a giant "loving light" and felt so comforting and kind. It felt like that's where I came from. After that I stopped worrying about my sanity. If this is crazy, I think it's a very good kind of crazy to be....

In loving light, Liane

Loving Light Books

Available at:
Loving Light Books: www.lovinglightbooks.com
Amazon: www.amazon.com
Barnes & Noble: www.barnesandnoble.com

Also Available on Request at Local Bookstores

www.ingramcontent.com/pod-product-compliance
Lightning Source LLC
La Vergne TN
LVHW091002080826
845145LV00003B/1092

9781878480088